D1216416

Making Economic Connections

Making Economic Connections

Larry Smith

Toronto

Canadian Cataloguing in Publication Data

Smith, Larry W. (Larry Wayne), 1945-
    Making economic connections

ISBN 0-13-093110-1

1. Economics.   I. Title.

HB171.5.S59 2002   330   C2001-903270-6

Copyright © 2002 Pearson Education Canada Inc., Toronto, Ontario

All Rights Reserved. This publication is protected by copyright, and permission should be obtained from the publisher prior to any prohibited reproduction, storage in a retrieval system, or transmission in any form or by any means, electronic, mechanical, photocopying, recording, or likewise. For information regarding permission, write to the Permissions Department.

Statistics Canada information is used with permission of the Minister of Industry, as Minister responsible for Statistics Canada. Information on the availability of the wide range of data from Statistics Canada can be obtained from Statistics Canada's Regional Offices, its World Wide Web site at **http://www.statcan.ca**, and its toll-free access number, 1-800-263-1136.

ISBN 0-13-093110-1

Vice President, Editorial Director: Michael Young
Executive Editor: Dave Ward
Marketing Manager: Deborah Meredith
Associate Editor: Pamela Voves
Production Editor: Julia Hubble
Copy Editor: Dawn Hunter
Production Coordinator: Patricia Ciardullo
Page Layout: Nelson Gonzalez
Permissions Research: Amanda McCormick
Art Director: Mary Opper
Interior and Cover Design: Anthony Leung
Cover Image: PhotoDisc

3 4 5   06 05 04 03

Printed and bound in Canada.

Table of Contents

II. Business Performance *31*

About the Author

Larry Smith is president of Essential Economics Corporation, a firm that serves a wide range of private and public clients and specializes in the economics of innovation and information technology. Educated at the University of Waterloo and the University of Western Ontario, Larry investigates the potential of new ventures and new technologies.

Larry Smith is an adjunct faculty member with the Department of Economics at the University of Waterloo, where he has taught more than 10 percent of UW's graduates. He is a recipient of the University of Waterloo's Distinguished Teacher Award and serves as an advisor to UW students who create their own ventures. He is a former adjunct professor at the Richard Ivey School of Business at the University of Western Ontario. He is a member of the President's Circle of the University of Waterloo, the Canadian Association for Business Economics, the Toronto Association for Business and Economics, and the Canadian Foundation for Economic Education, and he is associated with Shad International.

Acknowledgments

More people than can be named have contributed their insights to this work. First and foremost are my students, who taught me how to judge what was important to them and how to provide them with the tools they needed to succeed. Their generous response to applied introductory economics encouraged me to deepen the coverage of the course; their many suggestions and observations helped shape the content of this publication and its style of presentation.

The statistical research for this work was conducted in part by Christopher Bennett, who worked carefully and effectively. Christopher Poile completed the majority of the research. He met very tight timelines and quickly mastered multiple types and sources of data. His commitment to delivering quality data was obvious.

My colleagues in the Department of Economics at the University of Waterloo have provided both intellectual stimulation and wise counsel. The highest compliment is to acknowledge that I came to Waterloo for a brief sojourn and never left.

Gratitude is owed to my editors, David Ward, who was open to new approaches in educational publishing, and Pamela Voves, who helped me with the many practical challenges involved. The comments of the original reviewers were also much appreciated and highly useful. These reviewers included Dan Otchere, Concordia University; Martin Moy, University College of Cape Breton; and Ian Wilson, St. Lawrence College.

Very special thanks are due to Carolyn Holden for her administrative support. Her meticulous attention to detail was exemplary, as was her organization of this mass of data. While managing multiple responsibilities, she kept this project under control and on time. In particular, I value her consistently good cheer and encouragement.

Introduction

Making Economic Connections demonstrates how economic conditions are linked to personal and business success. It shows the connections between the pace of overall economic activity and the economic challenges faced by families, businesses, and society itself. By considering the sample of statistical evidence presented in this publication, you will come to a deeper understanding of longstanding economic principles. This understanding will help you to anticipate economic changes, allowing you to plan for the future more effectively and to discuss public policies with more insight.

The publication is organized into four themes:

I	**Economic Growth**
II	**Business Performance**
III	**Financial Markets**
IV	**Individual Success**

The principles relevant to Economic Growth and Financial Markets are found largely in textbooks on macroeconomics; the themes of Business Performance and Individual Success are found largely in textbooks on microeconomics. But economic understanding comes from integrating both macro and micro principles. Therefore, some of the units within each part are related to other parts, providing a comprehensive overview; real-world problems frequently cross academically defined boundaries. Each part has an introduction that establishes the framework, and each unit has a brief description of the relevant economic principle or concept. The specific principle or concept is in boldface type.

Do not look for this publication to provide neat and simple answers. Rather, it asks a sequence of important questions that arise from the selected evidence. The answers lie elsewhere. Some of the answers can be found in further research and in the analysis of economic principles outlined in the textbooks associated with this publication. Some of the answers lie within the presentations and lectures given by your instructor and in discussion with your instructors, classmates, and friends. Some of the answers can be found with thoughtful consideration of the questions. The answers may be complicated, but so is life.

Moreover, no answer is ever complete, and no *specific* answer is ever fixed in time. The statistical evidence presented here and in your textbooks is but a sliver of what is available, and new evidence is created every minute. Seek out additional and updated information. The websites of the world's principal statistical agencies, containing both data and commentary, are a mouse click away. There is no excuse for being ill informed or relying on someone else to tell you what to think. No one should ever listen to an argument, whether from a friend, businessperson, or public official, without requesting evidence, but only the well informed will know whether that evidence is accurate, complete, or relevant.

This publication invites you to embark on a continuing exploration of how economic principles shape society and its marketplace, and to use this accumulating knowledge to achieve your goals.

Part I: Economic Growth

The pace at which the economy's total production rises is one of the most powerful influences on the success of any individual, family, or business. All private and public purposes are supported by this production, whether for a new electronic device, for more medical research, or for a new office building. Any marked change in this pace sets off powerful cascading effects from the labour markets to the financial markets. To understand what causes these changes in the growth rate, it is necessary to watch it over time and in comparison to other countries. It is also necessary to focus on that part of the Canadian economy most responsible for its growth: foreign trade.

Gross Domestic Product

Economic activity can be analyzed by focusing on the summation of activity (**macroeconomics**) or on the economy's specific participants (**microeconomics**). The starting point for macroeconomics is the **gross domestic product (GDP)**, a measurement of the total value of final goods and services produced in one year. The rate of growth of the GDP is of great concern to the public authorities that manage **fiscal and monetary policy**, as well as to the financial markets and to individual businesses.

1. Who Says It Is Difficult to Forecast the Economy?
   The Rise of the Gross Domestic Product (GDP)
2. The Economy: 1981 to 2001
   Real GDP by Quarterly Change, at Annual Rates
3. Canada and the G7: Growth Rates
   Percentage Change in GDP, 1991–1999
4. The Economy: From the Great Depression to World War II
   Level of GDP Output and Percentage Change
5. What Does Canada Buy?
   GDP by Expenditure Share
6. The Sources of Canada's Income
   GDP by Income Share
7. How the Economy Adds Up
   GDP Expenditure and Income Bases, 2000

Industrial Sectors

While the GDP describes the overall state of the economy, it is also necessary to look at the **growth rates** of the principal industrial sectors. These sectors can grow at very different rates from the GDP. Some may outgrow the economy and others lag it for long periods. This results from the fact that the economy is adapting, devoting more of its resources to those endeavours where profits are expected to be higher. This adaptation is often connected with the **increasing demand** for new products or **technologies**.

Foreign Trade

The most important factor driving the growth of the **gross domestic product (GDP)** is Canada's success in selling its products to other countries **(exports)**, in particular to the United States. This success has allowed Canada to **import** an almost equally large number of products from other countries. Such imports make a major contribution to Canada's standard of living.

Part II: Business Performance

In a market economy, privately owned businesses produce the predominant share of **national output** (GDP) and **employment**. The widespread ownership of businesses through the stock market means that many people generate part of their wealth, not just their income, from the business sector. Many businesses, new and established, fail even as others are created, and many factors determine whether a business succeeds or fails in the marketplace. The strength of **demand**, the abundance of **supply**, the degree of **competition**, and the **public policy** environment are four of the most important. By understanding these factors, people can better plan their careers and investments. Otherwise, individuals, whether as employees or investors, are hostage to the skill of business leaders. It is always better to know than to hope.

Profit and Investment

A marketplace is driven by the pursuit of **profit**. Profit provides a promise of wealth to the business owners and is the necessary ingredient for **growth**. Profit naturally attracts resources, financial and real; **losses** imperil a company's survival. Profits and losses arise from many factors, such as **demand and supply conditions**, **competitive pressures**, and **knowledgeability**. Profit, for example, can result from delivering to the consumer a **highly valued product**, or from the consumer having to buy from a single seller (**monopoly**). Losses might result from a **shift in demand** away from the product or from inept management.

In spite of the central importance of profit as an encouragement to investment, the marketplace is also strongly affected by "**the urge to action, rather than inaction**" (John Maynard Keynes). This means, for example, that new enterprises are often created and grow based on the owner's sense of adventure, mission, or mania.

30. Who Makes More Profit: Canada or the United States?
    Total Profit as a Percentage of GDP
31. Profits in Canada and the United States: Detail
    Profit Share of GDP in Incorporated and Unincorporated Enterprises
32. Profit. Or Not!
    Revenues, Reported Profit, and Economic Value Added:
    Selected U.S. Companies
33. Where Does Business Investment Go?
    Business Investment by Expenditure Share of GDP

Prices

Prices are set by the conditions of **demand** and **supply** under **competitive conditions**. Prices, together with profit and losses, serve as a powerful signal to the marketplace about how **resources should be allocated**. In particular, prices are a rationing mechanism that is necessary since human **wants are unlimited** and the **resources** to satisfy these wants **are limited**. Of course, when production is allocated by price alone, social equity may not be served.

Cost of Business

Competitive marketplaces provide a powerful incentive for companies to gain advantage by lowering costs. In **highly competitive** marketplaces, lowering costs is essential to the survival of the business. Lower costs are, of course, a direct reflection of the efficient use of resources and their most appropriate **allocation among competing uses**. Frequently, businesses concentrate on increasing **output per worker** (see the unit on productivity). A company with a cost advantage over its competitors is usually in a strong position.

Lower costs also can allow for lower prices and thus benefit **consumers**. As well, reducing costs involves using fewer **scarce resources**, and this can ease pressure on the environment. Costs can be reduced through **effective management** and the appropriate use of **technology**, but managing **fixed** costs can be very different from lowering **variable** costs. **Public services** and **infrastructure** can also contribute to a cost-effective environment.

Entrepreneurship

Entrepreneurship is the act of creating a new venture and is often associated with **innovation**. **Entrepreneurial ventures** involve a significant commitment of **resources** and a lot of **risk**, and they usually take place over a long period. As entrepreneurs experiment with **new opportunities** in the marketplace and in **technology**, they play a vital role in helping an economy to **adapt**. As with any experiment, these ventures can fail, but it is often the newer company that introduces an innovation first—a common occurrence in the computer industry.

Technology

One of the most important sources of economic prosperity both for society and for individuals is the advance of **technology**: our **knowledge** of how to produce goods and services. As technology improves, **efficiency** increases and consumer **choice** expands. Thus, technology becomes a critical contributor to individual and collective **competitiveness**. An individual, company, or country that lags in technology is likely to suffer economic disadvantage.

Part III: Financial Markets

The financial markets facilitate the transfer of **money** and **financial assets** and by doing so provide the lubrication for all **marketplace transactions**. Since our society is now far too complex for widespread **barter exchange**, the prosperity of the **"real" economy** rests on the platform of a secure, smoothly functioning **financial system**. Some markets trade shares of ownership (**equity**) and others trade debt (**bond and money markets**).

Stock Markets

The stock markets trade shares that represent the ownership of the companies that have qualified for this privilege. The prices of the shares in these publicly traded companies rise or fall depending on both the **demand** for the shares and **supply** of them. The supply comes from investors who are selling previously issued shares and from companies who are issuing new shares to raise capital.

These **shares of ownership** represent a claim on the company's profits and the prices of these shares represent investors' judgment about how **profitable** the company is *and* how **profitable** it may be in the **future**. Since it is difficult, but not impossible, to forecast future profits, many investors make **mistaken investments** and incur considerable losses. That investors will often imitate each other adds to the danger of overreactions.

All factors that affect profitability are, of course, ultimately reflected in the stock market price. This includes both **microeconomic** issues, like the **strength of demand**, and **macroeconomic** concerns, like the **rate of interest**.

43. The Real and the Virtual
    The Toronto Stock Exchange: Price Index and Nominal GDP/Profit
44. The Great Tech Crash
    The NASDAQ Stock Price Index Close, End of the Month
45. What Makes the Market Move?
    Interest Rates and the North American Stock Markets

Interest Rates

Interest rates are a central tool of **monetary policy**, implemented by the **Bank of Canada**. Interest rates are affected by the **supply of and demand for loanable funds** and by the **supply of and demand for bonds**. Rising or falling rates can have a strong influence on the level of **aggregate demand** and in particular on the **desire to invest**. Sufficiently high interest rates can slow the rate of growth and can cause a **recession**. As a result, both the **equity** and **debt (bond) markets** are strongly affected by monetary policy.

46. What Makes Interest Rates Go Up or Down?
    The Money Supply (M1) and Interest Rates
47. How Much Did That Loan Really Cost?
    Real Interest Rates

Average Prices

Although individual prices rise and fall, the average price of what we buy for our **personal consumption** (**Consumer Price Index**) usually rises. Similarly, the average price of all the production of GDP (**GDP deflator**) usually rises. Rising average prices are described as **inflation**, and these price increases must be removed to measure **real GDP**. It is generally assumed that rising **inflation** (average prices rising at a faster rate) signals that the economy is approaching **its sustainable** level of production. **Monetary policy** response is expected in these circumstances.

Balance Sheet

Although much public comment is made about **debt**, public and private, much less attention is paid to **asset** holdings and the size of debts in relation to assets. Without such a context, the impact of debt cannot be properly assessed, nor can judgments be made about **wealth** (net worth). Yet wealth, both for individuals and for corporations, affects economic **confidence** and the **ability to borrow**, which in turn can affect **aggregate demand**.

Public Finances

The governments of Canada (federal, provincial, and municipal) represent a large sector of the economy. Although their size alone makes them influential, governments must serve a variety of mandates and resolve many of their conflicting responsibilities. Through **taxation**, they **redirect economic resources** away from some activities and toward others. **Governmental spending** shapes **social priorities** and funds the provision of **public infrastructure** among other things.

Public borrowing was very heavy in the past but is levelling off as governments balance their budgets. The governments' taxation and spending policies, together with the management of their debt, can have important effects on the rate of **GDP growth**, **business performance**, and the **financial markets**.

Part IV: Individual Success

Individual success requires a range of economic responses. With the support of family, the individual must choose both a career and an employer. The resulting household income must be spent wisely to ensure it is contributing to **welfare**, not **waste**. Finally, most households want to commit some of their resources to **investments** that will provide a source of **nonemployment income**. To make these decisions effectively, the individual must apply both **macroeconomic** and **microeconomic principles**. Of particular importance are the state of the **labour markets** and the **income flows** they generate.

Employment

While the GDP is the principal macroeconomic indicator, most people are more concerned with the state of the **labour markets**: how many people are **employed** and how many are **unemployed**. For most people, their work or their career is the source of most of their income and part of their sense of accomplishment. A powerful connection exists, of course, between employment and **standard of living**, and between employment and the rate of **GDP growth**. These connections, in turn, make employment a function of **aggregate demand conditions** and the conduct of **monetary and fiscal policy**. **Education** and **training** also play a role in the labour markets.

Productivity and Wages

Ultimately, Canada's **standard of living** is a function of productivity, or **output per worker**. Strictly speaking, productivity should measure **output per unit of time worked**, but this makes productivity difficult to measure since information on **number of hours worked** is becoming unreliable as relatively more people work in such unstructured occupations as professional practices and self-employment. This difficulty also makes comparisons among countries contentious. A variety of factors affect worker productivity, including **education**, **experience**, **technology**, and the workers' endowment of **capital goods** (plant, machinery, equipment, and public infrastructure). Wages are also ultimately linked to worker productivity.

Standard of Living

A principal way to evaluate an economy is to measure whether it increases **individual welfare**. Unfortunately, welfare cannot be measured directly, and it is also difficult to measure the factors that contribute to welfare or a **standard of living**. Such measures as **real GDP per person** or **real disposable income per person** have limitations, including the fact that they do not include **intangible values** or an allowance for the **distribution of income** among an economy's residents.

Part I: Economic Growth

The pace at which the economy's total production rises is one of the most powerful influences on the success of any individual, family, or business. All private and public purposes are supported by this production, whether for a new electronic device, for more medical research, or for a new office building. Any marked change in this pace sets off powerful cascading effects from the labour markets to the financial markets. To understand what causes these changes in the growth rate, it is necessary to watch it over time and in comparison to other countries. It is also necessary to focus on that part of the Canadian economy most responsible for its growth: foreign trade.

This part includes discussion of

- Gross Domestic Product
- Industrial Sectors
- Foreign Trade

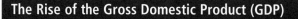

Figure **1**

Who Says It Is Difficult to Forecast the Economy?

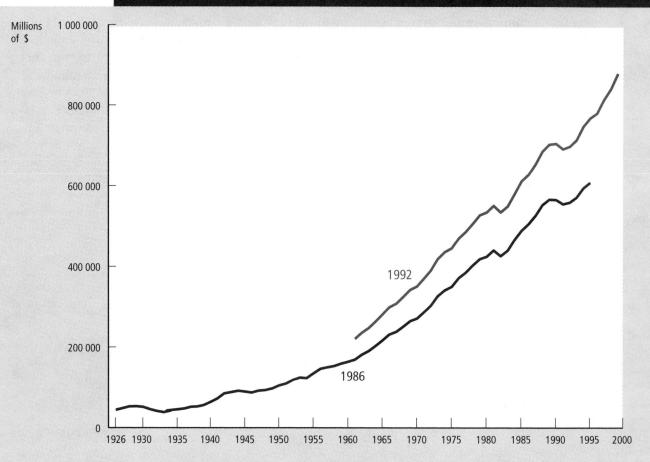

The Rise of the Gross Domestic Product (GDP)

Source: Statistics Canada/CANSIM (D14442, D22467)

The rate of economic growth is captured by **real gross domestic product (GDP)**, tracked over time. Real GDP measures the actual volume or amount of production, while nominal GDP is the dollar value of that production. Nominal GDP is affected by rising prices. The **GDP deflator** is used to correct for price changes. To provide an accurate comparison from 1926 to 1999, this figure uses two corrections, one set to 1986 prices and one set to 1992 prices. GDP growth is affected by the determinants of **aggregate demand**.

1. Since the end of World War II, how closely has the growth of the economy resembled a straight line?

2. To the extent that the economy grows in a linear projection, what happens to the average *rate* of growth?

3. Why does aggregate demand produce such powerful growth momentum?

4. How could this momentum help people to create *long-term* strategies for personal and business success?

Figure

2 The Economy: 1981 to 2001

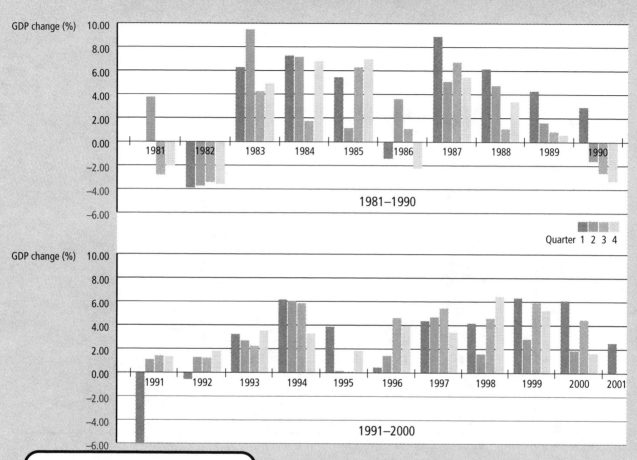

Real GDP by Quarterly Change, at Annual Rates

Source: Adapted from Statistics Canada/CANSIM (D100151).

The period from 1980 to today constitutes the economic life of many of today's post-secondary students. Several distinct events mark this period. In 1981–82 and 1990–91 there were **recessions** (defined as at least two consecutive quarters of contraction). The long expansions of the 1980s and 1990s were interrupted in 1986 and 1995, and the economy again slowed in 2001. The rhythm of these events is explained by the standard operation of **macroeconomic variables**, especially those of **monetary policy**.

1. What caused the recessions of 1981–82 and 1990–91? Did the same factor slow the economy in 1986, 1995, and 2001?

2. Why is the *underlying* trend of the economy to expand? What factors combine to produce this powerful forward momentum?

3. To what degree were the recessions, slowdowns, and expansions predictable?

3

Figure **3** Canada and the G7: Growth Rates

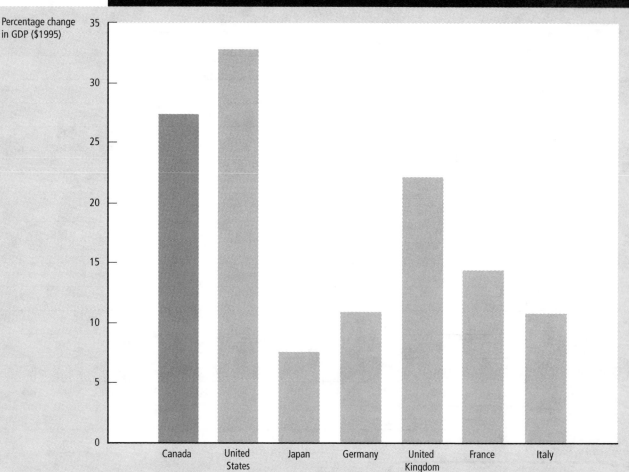

Percentage Change in GDP, 1991–1999

Percentage change in GDP ($1995)

Source: Organisation for Economic Co-operation and Development (OECD), *National Accounts of OECD Countries: Detailed Tables 1988/1998*, Volume 2, 2000.

The G7 countries have traditionally represented the leading economies of the industrial world. Although it is the smallest of the seven, Canada's critical importance to the U.S. economy justifies its inclusion. The key economies in the **European Union** (Germany, France, Italy and the United Kingdom) all had relatively solid growth during 1991 to 1999, with the United Kingdom outperforming the rest of them. Japan, once one of the most rapidly growing economies of the postwar period, underperformed all the G7. Characteristically, Canada's **growth rate** is relatively high, exceeded only by the United States in this period.

1. What factors may account for the North American economies outperforming the European nations of the G7? Why does the United Kingdom outperform its neighbours?

2. Are these differences in performance a function of both microeconomic and macroeconomic issues?

3. Why has Japan's economic performance changed so radically?

Figure 4 The Economy: From the Great Depression to World War II

Level of GDP Output and Percentage Change

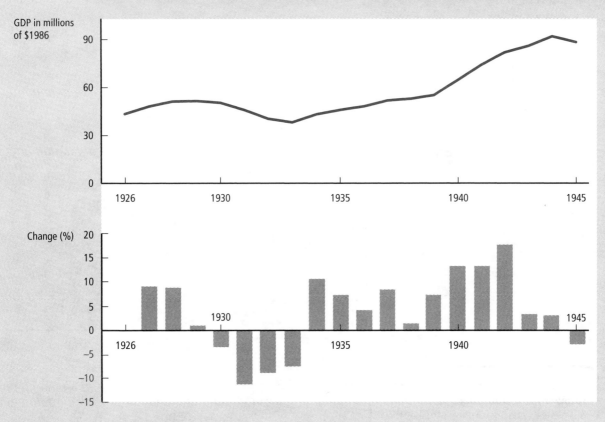

Source: Statistics Canada/CANSIM (D14442).

After strong growth in the 1920s, the **determinants of aggregate demand** seriously weakened. A prolonged period of economic contraction, called **the Great Depression**, occurred, causing great personal and business hardship and providing important lessons about **fiscal and monetary policy**. Recovery from the Depression was not completed until World War II began in 1939. Since then, economic growth has continued without such a severe contraction (see Unit 1) but with occasional **recessions** (see Unit 2).

1. What were the causes of the Great Depression? What prolonged it? Why did it end?
2. What was the economic role of World War II?
3. What is the likelihood that a contraction of a similar scale could occur again?

Figure 5 What Does Canada Buy?

GDP by Expenditure Share

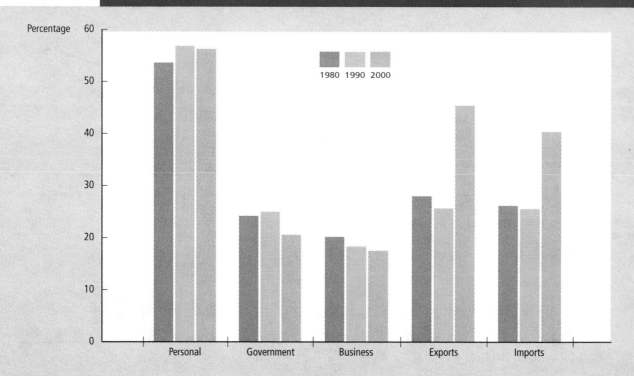

Percentage

1980 1990 2000

Personal Government Business Exports Imports

Source: Adapted from Statistics Canada/CANSIM (D14817, D14822, D14823, D14824, D14825, D14833, D14836, D14840).

Note: Amounts may not sum to 100 because of rounding; import share is subtracted.

The marketplace is designed to allocate both **resources** and **production**. As consumers, businesses, and government make their decisions to spend, the marketplace shifts its production accordingly. Some individuals or companies may drastically increase their **spending**, while others may reduce their **demand**. As a result, the expenditure shares change slowly over time. **Personal expenditures**, in particular, command a relatively stable share of GDP and claim the largest proportion of **GDP** (56.2 percent in 2000). Note that over the period presented, all levels of government in Canada have reduced their share of national production. The business sector's spending for **plant, machinery and equipment,** and **residential construction** also decreased. **Export** production, by contrast, increased drastically, as did spending on **imports** (which is subtracted from GDP expenditures since it is spending on another country's production), meaning that a larger share of Canada's consumer and business spending took advantage of foreign production.

1. Why did the export share of production rise so sharply?
2. Has the growth in imports contributed to Canada's standard of living?
3. Why did the governments of Canada reduce their relative share of expenditures? Why did the business sector do the same?

6 The Sources of Canada's Income

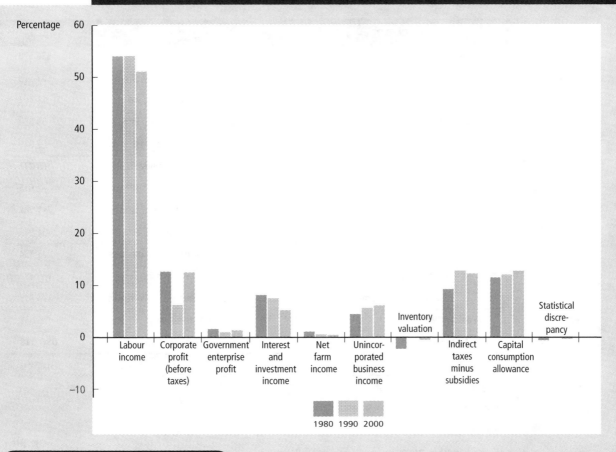

GDP by Income Share

Source: Adapted from Statistics Canada/CANSIM (Matrix 6520).

Note: Amounts may not sum to 100 because of rounding; import share is subtracted.

The marketplace generates a series of **income streams** from labour and from the ownership of productive resources. The share of GDP represented by each income stream changes over time, reflecting **economic conditions** and public policy decisions. From 1980 to 2000, the changes were significant. Labour income declined, while the corporate profit share fell sharply by 1990 and recovered by 2000. Interest and investment income also fell, while indirect taxes (less subsidies) rose. The very small discrepancy between GDP by expenditure share (Unit 5) and GDP by income share reflects the quality of these statistics.

1. Has the decline in the labour income share contributed to a change in economic confidence?

2. Why has unincorporated business income increased significantly?

3. Why did the governments of Canada decide to increase indirect taxes?

Figure 7

How the Economy Adds Up

GDP Expenditure and Income Bases, 2000

Expenditures	Millions of $		Income	Millions of $
Personal	593 275		Labour income	536 578
Government			Corporate profits before taxes	127 513
Current	192 771		Government enterprise profits	11 702
Investment			Interest and investment income	53 553
Fixed capital	24 740		Accrued net farm income	1 979
Inventories	24		Unincorporated business income	63 237
Business			Inventory valuation adjustment	−2 615
Investment	184 294		Net domestic income at factor cost	791 947
Residential construction	48 170		Taxes less subsidies on factors of production	54 949
Business investment	136 124		Taxes less subsidies on products	75 334
Non-residential	50 569		Indirect taxes, less subsidies	130 283
Machinery and equipment	85 555		Capital consumption allowances	134 315
Inventory change	7 144		Statistical discrepancy	−535
Non-farm	7 407		**GDP at market prices**	**1 056 010**
Farm	−263			
Exports	479 450			
Imports	426 223			
Statistical discrepancy	535			
GDP at market prices	**1 056 010**			

Source: Statistics Canada/CANSIM (Matrix 6520).

Source: Statistics Canada, CANSIM (Matrix 6521).

Accurate statistics about the **performance of the economy** are essential. Otherwise, private businesses cannot **plan effectively** and the public sector cannot implement **appropriate policies**. What you cannot measure, you cannot understand; what you cannot understand, you cannot anticipate. By measuring the economy according to both its **expenditure** and its **income** flows, the economy can be described from its two most fundamental perspectives: what you spend and what you earn. This statistical approach is based on the logic that **one dollar spent** creates **one dollar of income**. (What else could happen to it?) The actual size of the various expenditure and income flows also provides a comparative benchmark for all other economic transactions.

1. How can personal expenditures exceed labour income? (Are you sure that the answer is debt?)

2. What is the impact on the economy of a company that sells $10 billion worth of services and makes an $800 million profit?

3. What is the effect on the economy when the government spends $50 million unnecessarily?

4. Why does the capital consumption allowance represent so large a share of the income flow?

Figure **8** Physical or Not

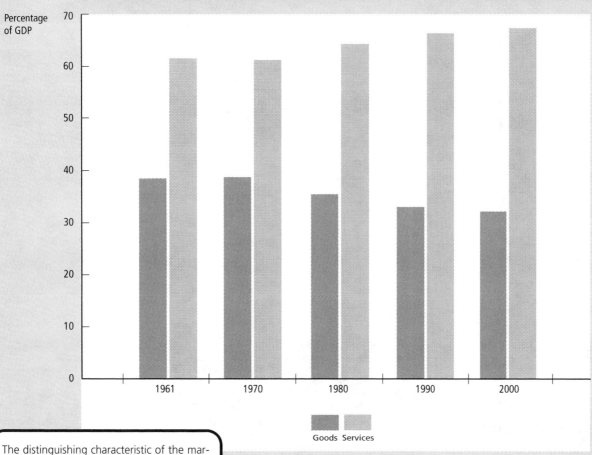

Goods and Services at Factor Cost as a Percentage of GDP

Percentage of GDP

Source: Adapted from Statistics Canada/CANSIM (Matrix 4678).

The distinguishing characteristic of the market is its **ability to adapt** to changing circumstances. Failure to adapt can have serious consequences. Between 1961 and 2000, the Canadian economy continued a very long cycle of adaptation as goods production declined in *relative* terms and service increased. This trend, common to other mature industrial countries, has alarmed some who believe that making a good, especially a **manufactured product**, results in "real" value, whereas producing a service, like an hour of health care, entertainment, or air travel, is inherently less valuable. However, the **market** defines value by rewarding it, and the market is plainly signalling that it values services. It is also a mistake to argue that manufactured goods are the foundation of an economy from which the **demand for services** arises.

1. Why is a manufactured good no more than just another product? Why are manufactured goods not the base on which the service economy advances?

2. What common factor results in most mature countries shifting toward service production?

3. Is the shift to service production slowing or accelerating? Why would this change occur?

9

Figure Computers and the Internet

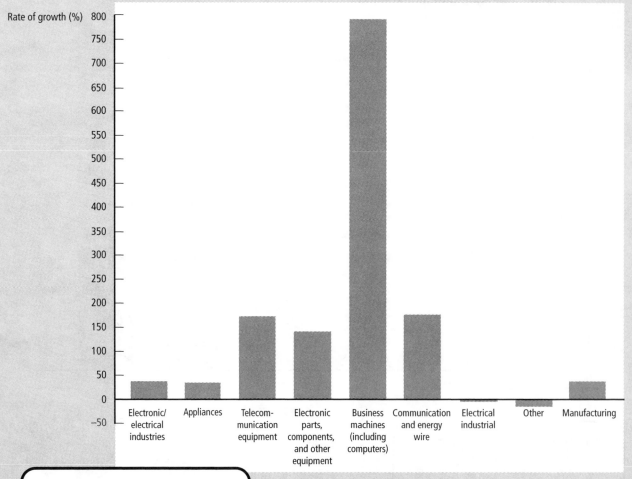

Electronics Production, Rate of Growth (at Factor Cost), 1990–2000

Rate of growth (%)

Source: Adapted from Statistics Canada/CANSIM (Matrix 4678).

The marketplace has long been fascinated by the potential of **information technologies**. In Canada and the United States, the computing, electronic, and communication industries have grown at extraordinary rates. This expansion resulted from **customer preferences**, **technological advances**, and the **willingness of the equity markets** to fund telecommunications in particular. Such rapid growth and the lure of **profit** (not surprisingly) attract many entrants, not all of whom are well prepared or well intentioned. An overreaction to the opportunities in this industry was almost inevitable. Unfortunately, hasty investment can **waste** resources as readily as a hesitant reaction can.

1. Can the past rates of growth of computer production be sustained?

2. What caused the very rapid growth of the telecommunications equipment industry to slow abruptly in 2000–01?

3. What is the long-term trend of the electronics and computer production?

4. Is there a difference in the growth potential of computing services compared to electronics/computer production?

Figure **10** # What We Make

Composition of Canada's Production at Factor Cost as a Percentage of GDP

Industry	1990 (%)	2000 (%)
Agriculture	1.87	1.65
Fishing, trapping, forestry	0.95	0.68
Mining, quarrying, and oil	3.53	3.49
Manufacturing	16.84	18.18
Construction	7.14	5.37
Transportation and storage	4.33	4.64
Communication and utility	6.59	7.17
Wholesale and retail trade	10.99	12.86
Finance, insurance, and real estate	15.04	16.08
Business services	4.80	6.31
Government services	7.13	6.00
Educational services	6.27	5.19
Health and social services	7.41	5.90
Accommodation, food, and beverage	3.02	2.67
Other	4.16	3.80

Source: Adapted from Statistics Canada/CANSIM (Matrix 4678).

Note: Amounts may not sum to 100 because of rounding.

A **marketplace-driven** economy is constantly shifting its resources to areas of growing opportunity. This **reallocation of resources** is sometimes not fully recognized since the movement of resources can be on a *relative* basis; that is, a sector may be growing but at a slower rate than another sector. Both sectors attract resources, but the faster-growing sector will attract resources at a higher rate. This important point is often missed by investors, who merely notice that a sector is growing, but they need to know the growth rate compared to other **equivalent alternatives (the principle of opportunity cost)**. Mistaken impressions about economic opportunities are made based on their alleged size. Size is a useful indicator only in comparison to other alternative activities. In spite of the public discussion about the rising costs of education and health care, both sectors decreased in relative size.

1. Why did the relative size of the manufacturing sector increase between 1990 and 2000?

2. How important is agriculture to Canada?

3. Why is the finance sector almost the size of manufacturing?

4. How does the relative size of the communication sector give an economic perspective to the Internet?

Figure 11

What's Hot? What's Not?

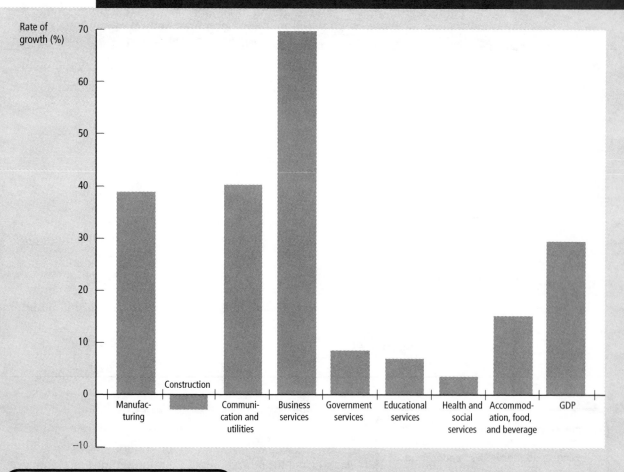

Industrial Growth at Factor Cost, Selected Industries, 1990–2000

The 1990s were marked by industrial production that varied dramatically among sectors. These differential growth rates reflect the **demand conditions** in individual markets, the **competitive strength** of the suppliers, and the **availability of resources**, both physical and financial. As always, technology shapes both the **demand** and the **supply** side. With GDP up 29.1 percent over the period, manufacturing output grew quickly. Although communications and utilities attracted interest, it only matched the pace of manufacturing. Business services, which includes computing services, grew much faster than communication and utilities, while health services expanded only modestly during the period. Health care and educational services each grew more slowly than did the economy.

Source: Adapted from Statistics Canada/CANSIM (Matrix 4678).

1. What factors caused government services to grow more slowly than GDP?

2. Can business services continue their current rate of expansion? (Consider the information in the previous unit.)

3. To what extent do these measurements reflect society's preferences and priorities?

Figure **12** Export Powerhouse

Exports as a Percentage of GDP

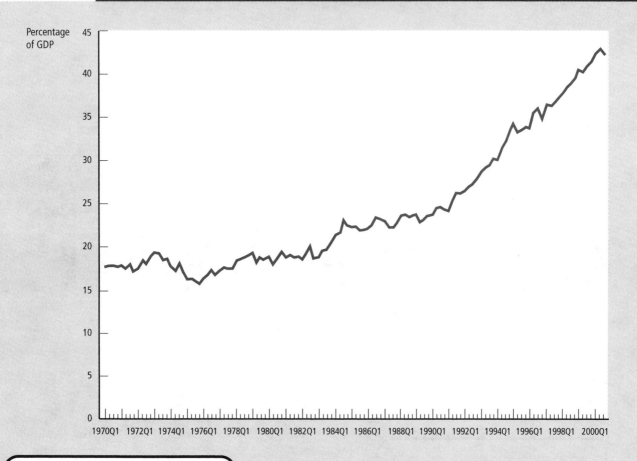

Percentage of GDP

Source: Adapted from Statistics Canada/CANSIM (Matrices 6521, 6540).

The **demand** for Canadian exports is driven by many factors, such as the importing country's economic **rate of growth**. This growth is in turn affected by the importing country's **credit conditions** and **fiscal policy**, including its ability to export. Equally important is the **exchange rate** between the Canadian currency and that of the importing country, the **rate of inflation**, and other **cost conditions** in Canada. A large volume of foreign trade makes Canada very sensitive to the terms of **international trade agreements**, such as those of the **World Trade Organization (WTO)**, **the General Agreement on Tariffs and Trade (GATT)**, and the **North American Free Trade Agreement (NAFTA)**.

1. What particular factors are responsible for the increase in Canada's exports? Does this reflect success and international competitiveness or some other circumstance?

2. Since Canada's exports have been increasing both in volume and in relative share of GDP, what *long-term* factors are at work?

3. Are the effects of Canada's international trade agreements apparent in these statistics?

Figure 13 World-Scale Exporter

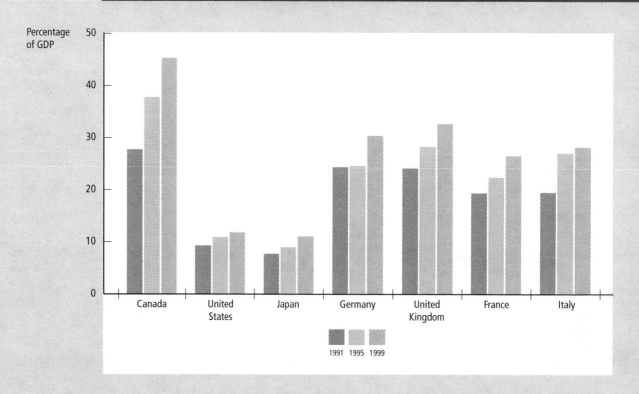

Exports as a Percentage of GDP, G7 Countries

Percentage of GDP

1991 1995 1999

Source: Organisation for Economic Co-operation and Development (OECD), *National Accounts of OECD Countries: Detailed Tables 1988/1998*, Volume 2, 2000.

Canada's *international* identity is well established: Its export performance has long been exceptional, and during the twentieth century, Canada outperformed the other G7 countries in relative terms. Although each country increased its **export orientation** as a percentage of GDP in the nineties, Canada gained the most by far. In 1991, Canada's export orientation was only a few percentage points higher than that of Germany and the United Kingdom. By 1999, Canada's lead had widened to almost 15 percentage points. This remarkable performance is the result of a variety of **macroeconomic** and **competitive variables**, both in Canada and in the other countries.

1. Why did all the G7 countries increase their exports?
2. What factors account for Canada's much greater increase?
3. Why is Japan's reputation as a successful exporter often better than Canada's?
4. Why might Canada's performance relative to the G7 countries change?

Figure 14 What Kind of Exports?

Exports of Goods and Services as a Percentage of Total Exports

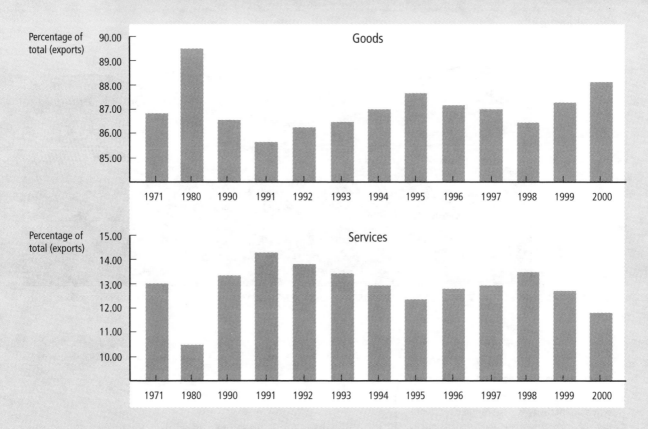

Source: Adapted from Statistics Canada/CANSIM (Matrix 6540).

Even though **service production** makes up the largest share of GDP, Canadian exports are largely **goods**. Since the **demand** for these exports has risen very sharply, they must have a **competitive advantage** over their production in other countries, which suggests that Canada has more of an international advantage in goods production than in service production. Indeed, the share of service exports has risen and fallen over this period in Canada; however, through the 1990s, service exports increased in value.

1. Are goods more "tradable" than services?
2. Why would the proportion of service exports fall, while the value rises?
3. Why would Canada have a greater competitive advantage in goods than in services?

Figure 15 Not Just Rocks and Trees

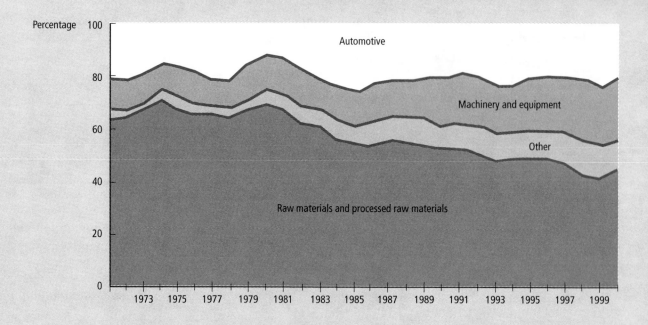

Shares of Merchandise Exports by Type

Source: Adapted from Statistics Canada/CANSIM (Matrix 0909).

One clear illustration of the Canadian economy's adaptability is the dramatic reorientation of its export base. Natural resources, both raw and processed, have been falling in *relative* terms for almost three decades. Automotive exports are approaching one-quarter of total exports. So, too, is machinery and equipment, the fastest growing sector. This long-term expansion of manufacturing exports has profoundly affected the **composition of Canada's exports** and consequently the **nature of the economy**.

1. Why have Canada's exports of natural resources fallen in relative terms? Why have Canada's exports of manufactured goods risen? How has the *volume* changed?

2. What part does the Canadian–U.S. exchange rate play in the growth of exports?

3. Why would this trend in exports continue? Why would it stop?

4. To what degree do Canada's exports reflect the use of technology, or are the exports technology?

Figure 16 Manufactured Diversity

Manufacturing Exports as Shares of Merchandise Exports by Type

Export	1980	1990	2000
Total motor vehicles and parts	14.20	22.81	23.06
Aircraft and parts	2.24	3.13	3.44
Other transportation equipment	1.29	1.29	1.34
Agricultural machinery	1.20	0.58	0.34
Communications and electronic equipment	2.67	5.57	8.24
Industrial machinery	3.25	3.47	4.03
Other equipment and tools	1.84	3.45	5.45
Other consumer goods	1.68	2.20	3.51
Other industrial goods	3.55	3.74	5.29
Total manufactured goods	31.92	46.23	54.70

Source: Adapted from Statistics Canada/CANSIM (Matrix 0909).

Not only has the manufactured goods' share of total merchandise exports sharply increased, the share of most main components has increased as well, including the "other goods" category. Canada's exports are at a record high in volume, as a proportion of GDP, in degree of manufacturing orientation, and in degree of diversification.

1. Why have Canadian automobile exports increased their relative share of manufactured exports?
2. What accounts for the significant increase in the diversification of Canada's manufactured exports?
3. To what degree do these exports represent technology-intensive products?
4. Why does Canada export relatively few consumer goods, excluding automobiles?

Figure **17** Not Just Snow

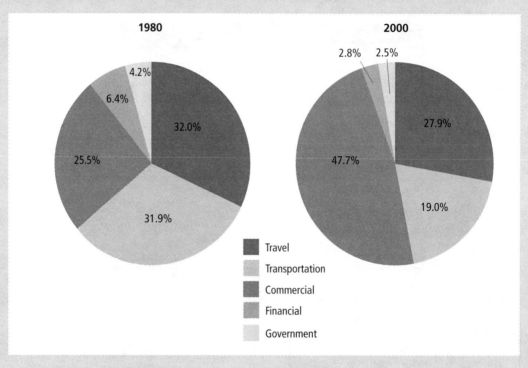

Service Exports by Category as a Percentage of Total Service Exports

1980

- 32.0%
- 4.2%
- 6.4%
- 25.5%
- 31.9%

2000

- 2.8%
- 2.5%
- 27.9%
- 47.7%
- 19.0%

Travel
Transportation
Commercial
Financial
Government

Source: Adapted from Statistics Canada/CANSIM (Matrix 6540).

Note: Amounts may not sum to 100 because of rounding.

The composition of Canada's service exports has changed considerably over this period. The value of service exports rose in several categories, but commercial services grew most strongly. Travel services, generated by tourists visiting Canada, transportation, government, and financial services faded in *relative* importance. The economy was therefore **adapting** according to changed **preferences** of foreign customers and shifts in Canada's **competitive advantages**. The growth of commercial services, including consulting, is desirable since it contributes to the **diversification** of service exports.

1. Why is it desirable to export a wider range of services rather than a narrower range?
2. What challenges does Canada face in its export of travel services, that is, in attracting tourists to Canada?
3. Why is the rapid growth of commercial service exports not particularly surprising?

Figure 18 Who Buys Canada's Goods?

Merchandise Exports by Country of Destination as a Percentage of Total Merchandise Exports			
Region	1980	1990	2000
United States	63.25	74.88	87.14
Europe	17.65	10.60	5.12
Asia	9.82	10.20	4.99
South America	3.17	0.93	0.74
Mexico	0.65	0.44	0.49
Other	5.46	2.95	1.52

Source: Adapted from Statistics Canada/CANSIM (Matrix 3686).

Over the past 20 years, Canada's merchandise exports have reached to record highs, and the United States has imported a sharply increasing share. This increase is the natural result of the size of the U.S. **marketplace**, the **affluence** of its consumers, its **proximity** to Canada, and a reflection of the fact that other regions, like Asia and Latin America, have experienced serious **macroeconomic stress**. Japan, for example, is growing far below its potential and historic norm. However, because so much of Canada's GDP is directed to the United States, Canada is acutely sensitive to the **willingness and ability of U.S. customers to buy**, which in turn is a function of the U.S. **rate of growth** and the **macroeconomic policies** of its public authorities.

1. If Canada wanted to expand its exports to areas outside the United States, why is Europe a logical choice?

2. How important is it to export to countries other than the United States?

3. What U.S. macroeconomic policies are presently affecting Canada's exports?

Figure 19

What Kind of Imports?

Imports of Goods and Services as a Percentage of Total Imports

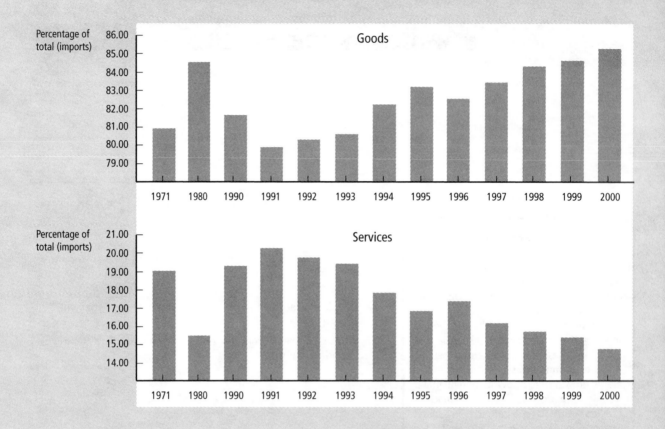

Source: Adapted from Statistics Canada/CANSIM (Matrix 6540).

Since the value of Canadian imports is only slightly less than the **value of its exports**, a large share of everything bought in Canada was produced in other countries. Although some mistakenly view this as a weakness, it merely demonstrates that having exported very large amounts, especially to the United States, Canada receives its payment as imports. The imports are, in effect, what Canada buys from the proceeds of its exports. Like the export flow, the bulk of imports are goods rather than services; the proportion of imports is at a record high for the period.

1. Why does Canada export a higher proportion of goods than it imports?

2. In what circumstances would it be economically appropriate to replace imports with domestic production?

3. Why did the proportion of service imports fall in the late 1990s?

Figure **Retail Imports?**

Merchandise (Goods) Imports by Category as a Percentage of Total Merchandise Imports

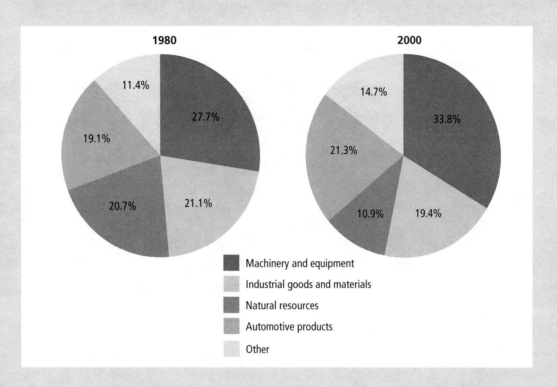

1980

27.7%
11.4%
19.1%
20.7%
21.1%

2000

33.8%
14.7%
21.3%
10.9%
19.4%

■ Machinery and equipment
□ Industrial goods and materials
■ Natural resources
■ Automotive products
□ Other

Source: Adapted from Statistics Canada/CANSIM (Matrix 6540).

Note: Amounts may not sum to 100 because of rounding.

As merchandise import values rose, the composition of these imports changed. The percentage of natural resource imports was almost halved, while the percentage of automotive imports and industrial goods and materials remained stable. The "other" category showed a clear increase, and the percentage of imports in the machinery and equipment category increased the most. Since machinery and equipment embody **technology**, Canada was importing more technology in 2000 than in 1980. In spite of the range of imported goods in most Canadian stores, **consumer goods** in the automotive and "other" categories constituted less than 40 percent of all merchandise imports.

1. Why was Canada importing relatively more machinery and equipment in 2000?

2. Why are the bulk of Canada's imports directed to business needs rather than to personal consumption?

3. Why have automobile imports remained relatively stable?

Figure 21 Consultants or Sunshine?

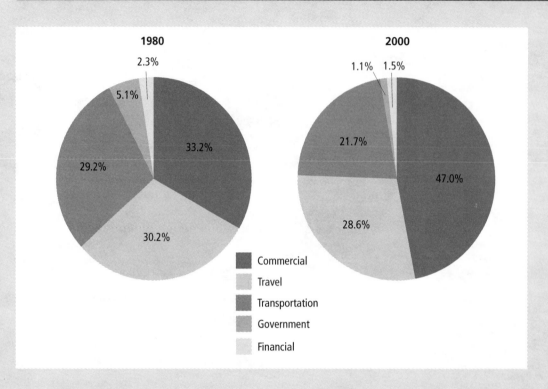

Service Imports by Category as a Percentage of Total Service Imports

Source: Adapted from Statistics Canada/CANSIM (Matrix 6540).

Note: Amounts may not sum to 100 because of rounding.

The composition of Canada's service imports has changed sharply. Travel imports, Canadians visiting other countries, and transportation, government, and financial services all fell. Commercial service imports increased strongly, representing almost half of service imports in 2000. This increase reflects the rising importance of the **business services sector** to the economies of Canada and the United States and provides additional evidence of how the overall economy **adapts** to the changing **structure** of economic activity.

1. What role do Canada's commercial service imports play in the operation of the economy?
2. Does the rapid increase in commercial service imports reflect a lack of international competitive advantage in Canada?
3. Why has Canadians' desire for foreign travel diminished?

Figure **22** Who Supplies Canada's Imported Goods?

Merchandise Imports by Country of Origin as a Percentage of Total Merchandise Imports

Region	1980	1990	2000
United States	68.49	64.52	64.35
Asia	7.68	13.61	13.88
Europe	10.69	14.84	12.53
South America	1.02	0.73	1.36
Mexico	0.49	1.28	3.39
Other	8.28	5.02	4.49

Source: Statistics Canada/CANSIM (Matrix 3887).

In this period, Canada's merchandise imports reached record highs, and the United States remained Canada's largest supplier of foreign goods. However, the United States' relative share eroded somewhat. Mexico and Asia both increased their share significantly; non-American suppliers are providing goods at a **price** and **quality** not available from the United States—that is, they have found new sources of **competitive advantage**. The growing importance of Mexico as a supplier may be a consequence of the public policies designed to create an integrated North American marketplace.

1. Does the growth in imports from non-American suppliers necessarily reflect a decline in U.S. competitiveness?

2. In what ways does the North American Free Trade Agreement (NAFTA) help Mexico sell more to Canada and to the United States?

3. Why did Europe's share of Canada's imports fall between 1990 and 2000?

Figure 23 Where Does Canada Stand?

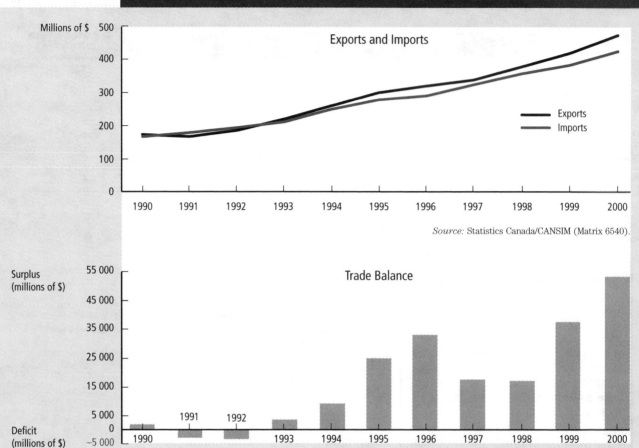

Foreign Trade Balance

Exports and Imports

Millions of $

Source: Statistics Canada/CANSIM (Matrix 6540).

Trade Balance

Surplus (millions of $)

Deficit (millions of $)

Source: Statistics Canada/CANSIM (Matrix 6540).

Note: The trade balance is negative when imports exceed exports (deficit)

A persistent trade imbalance, *either* a **surplus** or a **deficit**, can be a signal that an economy is engaged in an **unsustainable** course of action. A continuing trade deficit must be funded by a capital inflow, and a trade surplus necessitates a capital outflow. In both cases, a country becomes vulnerable to a change in the **perspectives** of domestic or foreign investors. The **capital markets** are subject to volatility, and they are particularly affected by **macroeconomic policies**. Canada's trade surplus has risen sharply in the past few years, suggesting a change in the underlying determinants of the country's exports or imports.

1. What circumstances in Canada could have caused the trade balance to rise sharply?
2. What circumstances in the United States, Canada's principal trading partner, might have changed?
3. Is Canada's large trade surplus likely to continue?

Figure 24 Trade Balance: Detail

Selected Foreign Trade Balances, 2000

Categories	(Millions of $)		
	Export	Import	Balance[1]
Goods and services	479 450	426 223	53 227
Goods	422 562	363 278	59 284
Services	56 888	62 945	−6 057
Selected categories			
Travel services	15 897	18 030	−2 133
Commercial services	27 140	29 594	−2 454
Selected countries			
United States	359 155	229 513	129 642
Europe	21 122	44 699	−23 577
Asia	20 566	49 513	−28 947

Source: Statistics Canada/CANSIM (Matrices 6540, 3887, 3686).

Note 1: The trade balance is negative when imports exceed exports (deficit).

Canada's trade balances are marked by a distinct pattern: large surpluses in some categories or countries and large deficits in others. The result produces an overall trade surplus, a large one recently, and these dramatic differences in our trading relationships invite inquiry. Canada's **competitive advantages**, in light of foreign customers' preferences, facilitate the export of goods over services. It is easier, for example, to sell Canadian goods than commercial or travel services. It also appears easier to sell to the United States than to Europe or Asia—or maybe Europeans simply want to buy more from the United States than from Canada.

1. Are there economic advantages to Canada if its trade is more evenly balanced among categories and countries?
2. Are there political advantages if trade is more evenly balanced?
3. Why would Europeans be reluctant to buy from Canada and Americans not?
4. Are these differences in trade preference no more than the result of comparative advantage?

25
Figure

Money In/Money Out

Canada's Balance of International Payments

	Current Account	Capital/Financial Net Flow	Statistical Discrepancy	Balance[1]
		(Millions of $)		
1980	−7 120	6 979	142	0
1981	−14 994	19 423	−4 429	0
1982	2 302	−28	−2 274	0
1983	−3 132	6 506	−3 373	0
1984	−1 673	8 967	−7 294	0
1985	−7 828	13 659	−5 831	0
1986	−15 514	17 416	−1 902	0
1987	−17 806	20 869	−3 063	0
1988	−18 328	17 817	511	0
1989	−25 812	27 617	−1 806	0
1990	−23 135	25 167	−2 032	0
1991	−25 629	25 791	−162	0
1992	−25 360	21 890	3 470	0
1993	−28 093	34 467	−6 374	0
1994	−17 730	17 762	−32	0
1995	−6 099	1 294	4 805	0
1996	4 600	−12 234	7 633	0
1997	−11 397	15 764	−4 367	0
1998	−12 277	4 964	7 312	0
1999	1 690	−12 009	10 318	0
2000	26 894	−15 164	−11 730	0

Source: Statistics Canada/CANSIM (D58032, D58048, D58071).

Note 1: Amounts may not equal zero because of rounding.

Canada's balance of international payments describes the financial transactions between Canada and the rest of the world. The **current account** measures the effect of Canada's imports and exports, plus the payment of interest and dividends to other countries and their payments to Canada. The capital and financial net flow measures the effect of Canada's purchase of foreign assets and the world's acquisition of Canadian assets. A negative entry means that on balance Canada is paying more than it is receiving (**deficit**); a positive entry means that Canada is receiving more than it is paying (**surplus**). Since the amount of foreign currency Canada uses for foreign payments must equal the amount of foreign currency available to Canada, the balance of payments must logically sum to zero. To the extent that it does not, the **statistical discrepancy** measures the value of the transactions that are unaccounted for.

1. Why has the current account, usually in deficit, become a surplus in recent years? Why has the capital and net financial flow gone from a surplus to a deficit?

2. What does the relative size of the statistical discrepancy suggest? What kinds of transactions are most likely to be unaccounted for?

3. How does the balance of payments help explain the exchange rate between the Canadian and U.S. dollar?

Figure 26 Array of Relationships

Current Account Detail, 2000

	Payment of Non-residents to Canada (Millions of $)	Payment to Non-residents by Canada (Millions of $)	Balance[1] (Millions of $)
Goods and services	477 850	−425 286	52 564
Investment income	42 336	−69 458	−27 121
Transfers	6 043	−4 591	1 452
Current account total	526 229	−499 335	26 894

Source: Statistics Canada/CANSIM (Matrix 2360).

Note 1: Amounts may not sum exactly because of rounding.

The composition of Canada's current account is very distinctive, with a large surplus on the international **trade in goods and services**, and a large deficit on **investment (interest and dividends) income**. Overall, Canada had a surplus in 2000, an unusual outcome in the past 20 years. The surplus comes from a very sharp increase in the surplus on the trade in goods, since trade in services produces a deficit. The investment income account has long been in deficit.

1. What does the current account say about the present state of the Canadian economy?
2. Does the current account suggest that Canada is particularly vulnerable to outside events? What kinds of events?
3. Is the current account surplus going to last?
4. Why is the investment income flow negative?

Figure 27

Buying and Selling Assets

Capital Account and Financial Flows Detail, 2000

	(Millions of $)	
Capital account[1]		
Capital inflow	6 003	
Capital outflow	−741	
Total net flow	5 261	5 261
Canadians acquiring foreign assets		
Direct investments	−65 415	
Portfolio	−62 677	
Other	−1 331	
Official reserves	−5 480	
Total net outflow	−134 903	−134 903
Foreigners acquiring Canadian assets		
Direct investments	94 059	
Portfolio	19 647	
Other	771	
Total net inflow	114 477	114 477
Total capital and financial net flow		−15 164

Source: Statistics Canada/CANSIM (Matrix 2360).

Note 1: Miscellaneous transfers.

The capital and net financial flow transactions reveal that Canadians are making very large investments in foreign assets, and foreigners are acquiring a large volume of Canadian assets. These include **direct investments** in which the purchaser will control the investment, and **portfolio investments** in which the purchaser acquires stock or bonds and has no control. These investments are affected by the **expectation of future returns**. This expectation is in turn affected by existing **interest rates** and **profitability**. Investors should also consider the effects of **public policy** and the **expected growth rate** of the overall economy.

1. Why does the world undertake a higher level of direct investment in Canada than Canada makes in the world?

2. By contrast, why do Canadians undertake a much higher level of portfolio investment in the world than the world does in Canada?

3. What do these figures say about Canada's perception of the rest of the world and the world's perception of Canada?

4. What role do the "official reserves" play?

Catching Up

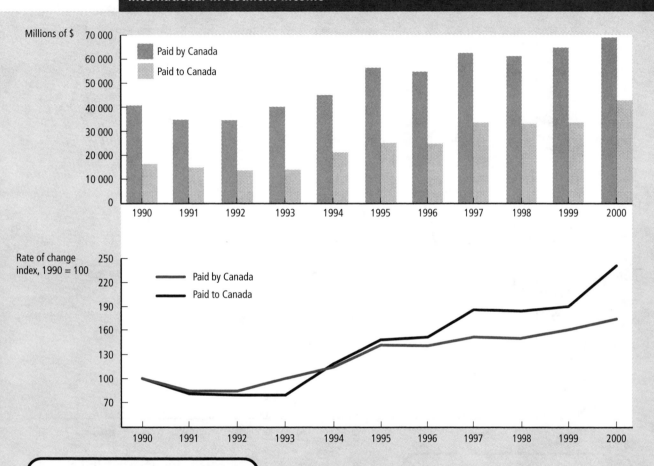

International Investment Income

Millions of $

Legend:
- Paid by Canada
- Paid to Canada

(Bar graph, 1990–2000, y-axis 0 to 70 000)

Rate of change index, 1990 = 100

Legend:
- Paid by Canada
- Paid to Canada

(Line graph, 1990–2000, y-axis 70 to 250)

Source: Adapted from Statistics Canada/CANSIM (D58009, D58025).

Since the deficit in international investment income has a major effect on the **balance of international payments**, and therefore on the **exchange rate** between the Canadian and U.S. dollar, it is important to trace its change over time. The first graph shows that payments in both directions are rising, but payments to Canada are rising faster than payments made by Canada, so the relative imbalance is declining. The differences in the rate of change are presented in the second graph. If these trends continue, the consequences for the balance of payments and exchange rate may be considerable. A variety of factors can affect this shift, from the **willingness of Canadians** to invest outside the country to the relative **rates of growth** of the economies in which the investments are held.

1. Why did investment income both into and out of Canada decline in the early 1990s?

2. Why did payments to Canada fall more sharply than did the payments Canada made to others in the early 1990s?

3. Why did the investment income payments received by Canada rise faster than the equivalent payments to the world?

4. What would cause this trend to continue? To reverse?

Figure 29 Downward Dollar?

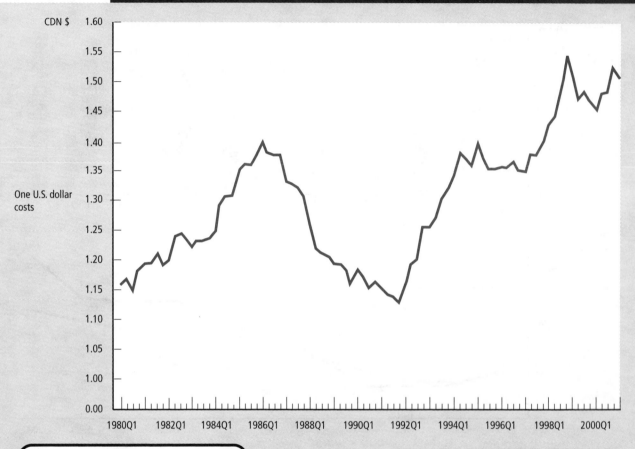

Canada–U.S. Exchange Rate by Quarters

Source: Statistics Canada/CANSIM (B3400).

Note: One U.S. dollar in Canadian dollars.

The Canada–U.S. exchange rate is the price of the Canadian dollar in U.S. dollars or the price of the U.S. dollar in Canadian dollars (pictured above); like all prices, it is a function of the supply of Canadian dollars offered to international **financial intermediaries** and the foreign demand for Canadian dollars. Alternatively, it is the Canadian **demand for foreign currency** and the **supply of foreign currencies** offered by non-Canadians. Canadians use foreign currencies to buy foreign products (Canada's **imports**) and acquire foreign assets (**capital outflow from Canada**). Non-Canadians use Canadian currency to buy Canadian products (**Canada's exports**) and to acquire Canadian assets (**Canada's capital inflow**). Thus, the exchange rate reflects indirectly these **trade *and* capital flows**. The exchange rate does not directly reflect the strength or prosperity of the economy.

1. How do the factors that affect trade flows differ from those that affect capital flows?

2. In what ways are capital flows affected by noneconomic events, like a political development in another country?

3. Why is the exchange rate an unreliable indicator of whether the purchasing power of the average Canadian is rising or falling? By contrast, why is the Consumer Price Index a reliable measurement with respect to whether the typical Canadian is getting "richer" or "poorer"?

Part II: Business Performance

In a market economy, privately owned businesses produce the predominant share of national output (GDP) and employment. The widespread ownership of businesses through the stock market means that many people generate part of their wealth, not just their income, from the business sector. Many businesses, new and established, fail even as others are created, and many factors determine whether a business succeeds or fails in the marketplace. The strength of demand, the abundance of supply, the degree of competition, and the public policy environment are four of the most important. By understanding these factors, people can better plan their careers and investments. Otherwise, individuals, whether as employees or investors, are hostage to the skill of business leaders. It is always better to know than to hope.

This part includes discussion of

- Profit and Investment
- Prices
- Cost of Business
- Entrepreneurship
- Technology

Figure

Who Makes More Profit: Canada or the United States?

Total Profit as a Percentage of GDP

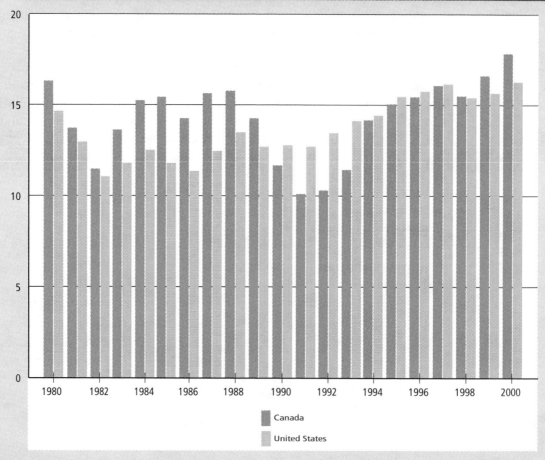

Total profit as percentage of GDP

Source: Adapted from Statistics Canada/CANSIM (D14816, B51100, B51105, B51102, D14806, D14810).

The share of profit business owners earn, expressed as a percentage of GDP, is an important indicator of the ability of the private marketplace to grow. Many factors affect this allocation of profit, including **market structure**, **competitive conditions**, **cost conditions**, and the strength of **demand** in various sectors. Although it is commonly asserted that Canada is a "poor" place to do business or that it is becoming similar to the U.S. marketplace, the profit shares of Canadian enterprise differ markedly from those in the United States.

1. What factors explain why Canadian enterprises have recently taken a larger profit share of national income than have U.S. enterprises of their country's national income?

2. Why did Canada's profit performance lag in the early part of the 1990s and return to its former position after that?

3. How is the competitive environment in Canada different from that of the United States? Has anything caused the competitive conditions to change?

Figure **31** Profits in Canada and the United States: Detail

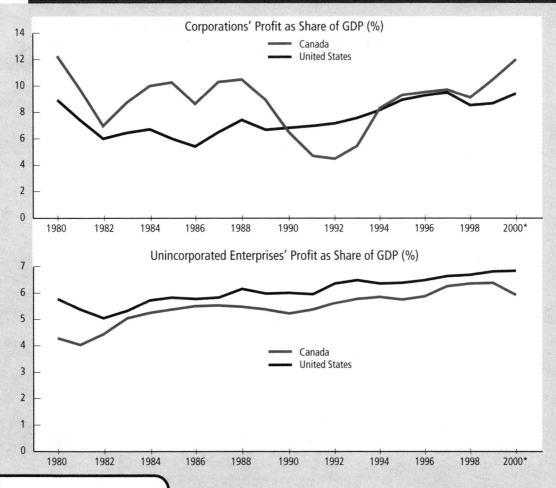

Profit Share of GDP in Incorporated and Unincorporated Enterprises

Source: Adapted from Statistics Canada/CANSIM (D14816, B51100, B51105, B51102, 14806, D14810).

* Based on the first three quarters of 2000.

Profits are generated by two different types of enterprises. **Corporations**, having been **incorporated** by the state, have the rights of natural persons. Consequently, these corporations can own property, borrow money, enter into contracts, and need never to be terminated. They shelter investors from the corporation's liabilities, which allows the company to grow and to conduct business over long periods. In doing so, they may be able to capture **economies of scale**. Shares in corporations may be **publicly traded** on the stock markets or be **privately held** by a limited number of persons. Other enterprises are unincorporated and are the direct property of their owners. The share of profit going to these two types of enterprise varies significantly in Canada and the United States, and between the two countries.

1. What factors account for a larger share of GDP going to corporate profits in Canada compared to the United States?

2. What do the profit share numbers say about the attractiveness of Canada as a place to invest?

3. Why is the profit share going to unincorporated Canadian businesses smaller than in the United States? What factors account for a larger share of profit going to Canadian corporations instead of to Canadian unincorporated businesses?

Figure 32 Profit. Or Not!

Revenues, Reported Profit, and Economic Value Added for Selected U.S. Companies

Company	Revenues[1]	Reported Accounting Profit[2]	Economic Value Added[3]
		Billions of U.S.$	
AT&T	62.39	3.43	**−6.38**
Boeing	57.99	2.31	**−0.83**
Coca Cola	19.80	2.43	1.56
Cisco Systems	12.15	2.10	0.18
Compaq Computer	38.52	0.59	**−1.20**
Ford Motor	162.56	7.24	5.42
General Motor	176.56	6.00	0.17
Hewelett Packard	48.25	3.49	**−0.19**
IBM	87.55	7.71	1.35
Intel	29.39	7.31	4.69
Microsoft	19.75	7.78	5.80
Motorola	30.93	0.82	**−1.17**
Pepsico	20.37	2.05	**−0.44**
Sun Microsystems	11.72	1.03	0.59
Wal-Mart Stores	166.81	5.38	1.53
WorldCom	37.12	4.01	**−4.74**

Source: Data are from the Stern Stewart Performance 1000, as reported in *Fortune*, 24 July 2000 and 18 December 2000, pp. 208–216.

Notes: 1: Sales revenues for the fiscal year ending 31 March 2000.
2: Reported earnings, after taxes, according to generally accepted accounting principles, for the fiscal year ending 31 March 2000.
3: Net operating profit after tax, less a charge for capital used (related to the return from an equally risky investment) for 1999.

Profit is the essential measurement of business performance. **Profit** is the **signal for resources to move**, to enter or to leave an industry or endeavour. When companies or investors disregard profits, as they did in the great explosion of "dot-com" enterprises, considerable economic damage will result (as it did). Like all economic measures, profit must be calculated with great care. Unfortunately, many investors and businesses concentrate on **accounting profits**, rather than on carefully defined **economic profits**, but *ultimately* economic profits drive the marketplace.

1. Why does the relationship between revenue and reported profit vary so much from company to company? Why does Ford report higher profit even though its revenues are less than General Motors?

2. Why does economic value added vary so much among the companies? How can WorldCom have positive reported profit and negative economic value added?

3. Why should stock market investors pay attention to economic value added?

4. How similar is economic value added to the formal definition of economic profit?

Figure 33 Where Does Business Investment Go?

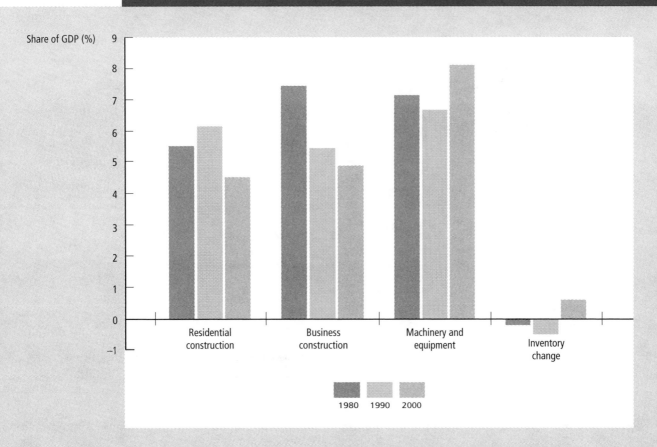

Business Investment by Expenditure Share of GDP

Source: Adapted from Statistics Canada/CANSIM (D14826, D14828, D14829, D14830).

Residential construction is part of the "investment" category of GDP because it creates a long-term asset, but houses do not, of course, increase the **productive capacity** of the economy the way expenditures on **business construction** (plants and offices) and on **machinery and equipment** do. During the period indicated, both residential and business construction reduced their share of GDP expenditures. By contrast, spending on machinery and equipment increased its share significantly.

1. What demographic reason might account for the decline in the share of GDP expenditures devoted to residential construction?

2. What factors are causing the share of GDP expenditures going to business construction to fall and the share of machinery and equipment GDP expenditures to rise? What role is technology playing?

3. How does business investment increase the productive capacity of the economy?

Figure 34 Is the Internet Affecting U.S. Retail Prices?

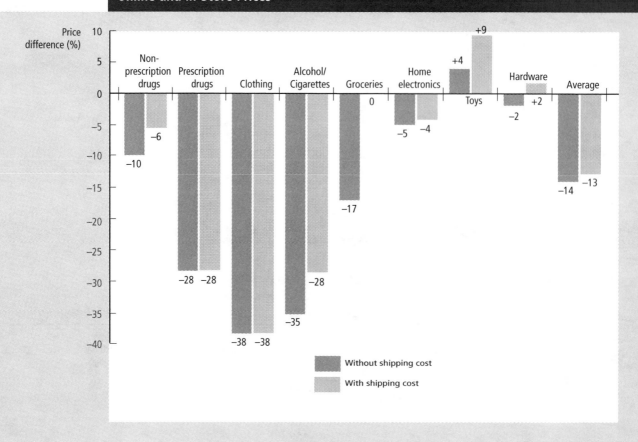

Online and In-Store Prices

Source: Data are from a Lehman Brothers survey, as reported in *Business Week*, 4 October 1999.

Note: A negative value means that the online price is lower.

The Internet as an inexpensive communication tool makes it easier for buyers and sellers to talk and to trade; thus, it greatly expands the scope of any **marketplace**. Since the Internet attracts more sellers, it should make the marketplace more **competitive**, with consequent effects on **cost and price**. But when the Internet is used to sell goods directly from a central location (e-commerce) rather than from traditional stores, shipping costs become an especially important factor.

1. Why does the difference between online and in-store prices vary so much depending on the product category? Degree of competition? Demand conditions?

2. Why do some categories appear to be more influenced by shipping costs than do others?

3. What is likely to happen to this difference between online and in-store prices over time?

Figure **35** Truck Mania?

Manufacturers' Suggested Retail Price of Cars and Trucks

	1994	2000	% Change
Trucks[1]	$17 851	$26 632	+49.2
Cars[2]	17 578	21 381	+21.6
Price difference	273	5 251	

Source: Adapted from DesRosiers Automotive Consultants, *The Globe and Mail*, 13 June 2001.

Notes: 1: Includes pickups, minivans, and sport utilities (SUV) weighted by sales.
2: Weighted by sales.

The relative price of trucks, compared to cars, rose sharply. A change in **relative price**, the price of one product compared to another, signals changes in the **demand** or **supply** conditions affecting that product. The **demand** curve is affected by such issues as changes in **tastes and preferences** or the **rate of growth of the population**. **Supply** is affected by the **state of technology** or increases in the cost of the **factors of production**.

1. What might have caused consumers' preference for trucks, minivans, and SUVs to increase? Or did the preference for cars fall and that for trucks stay the same?
2. Was there a difference in costs that would have affected supply?
3. Why would consumers, who live largely in cities, have a strong desire for vehicles designed for rural or wilderness areas?

Figure 36 eToys

Revenues and Costs at a "Dot Com," 1999

Sales Revenue for eToys[1]	For each $100	
Cost of		
Toys and shipping	$ 81	
Website and technology	29	
Labour for handling and parking	33	
Advertising	37	
Total cost	180	−180
Net Loss		−$80

Source: Adapted from *Fortune*, 18 September 2000.

Notes: 1: Online retailer of toys.

Online retailing has attracted a lot of interest and with the **barriers to entry** relatively low, many companies have entered (and left) this marketplace. The promise of **profit** attracted a very large commitment of resources, although many companies found it very difficult to achieve that profit. Apart from the **microeconomic** challenges, a tighter **monetary policy** slowed overall economic activity in 1999.

1. Which costs are variable? Which costs are fixed?
2. How might costs be lowered?
3. What factors affect a company's ability to raise prices?
4. Why did investors provide so much money to companies like eToys?
5. Why were investors once attracted to this stock? (During 1999, the stock price hit a high of just over $80; on 12 January 2001, eToys' share price was 18¢. In March 2001, eToys declared bankruptcy.)

Where Is It Cheaper to Run a Business?

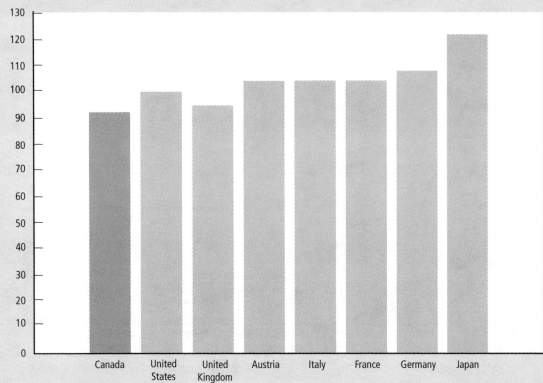

Total Annual Costs Index, All Industries

Annual cost index (U.S. = 100)

Source: World Competitiveness Yearbook, June 2000, p. 369. Prepared by the International Institute for Management Development, Lausanne, Switzerland.

The North American Free Trade Agreement (NAFTA) is creating an integrated market among Canada, the United States, and Mexico. It is important, therefore, to know whether Canadian enterprise has a systemic **cost disadvantage** compared to the United States, Canada's principal foreign marketplace. Of course, cost conditions in individual industries vary greatly.

1. Why is it cheaper to do business in Canada than in the United States?

2. What must Canada do to sustain this advantage?

3. What are sources of cost disadvantages?

Figure **38** Health Cost Burden on U.S. Business

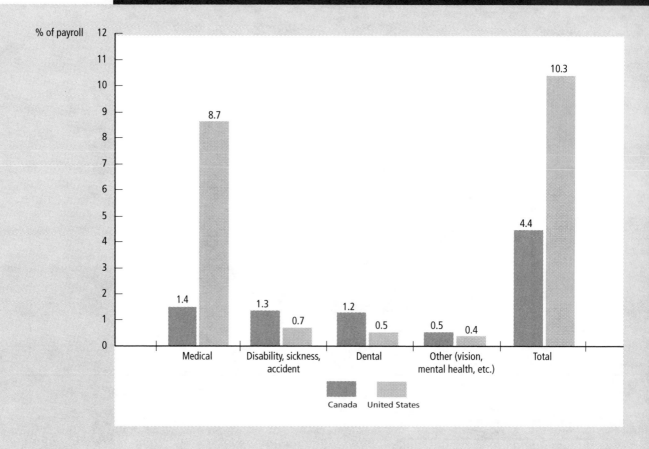

Health Benefits as a Percentage of Annual Payroll, 1995–1997

Source: *Employee Benefits*, US Chamber of Commerce, 1995, and *Global Competitiveness Report*, KPMG Management Consulting, 1997.

Everyone understands that government-provided **public goods**, such as transportation infrastructure, are essential for private businesses to operate **efficiently**, and that publicly supported **education** is indispensable to the supply of skilled labour. However, the government's **social policies**, such as for health care, are often not seen as contributing to private sector efficiency, although they do.

1. Why is the payroll burden so much higher in the United States?

2. What accounts for the fact that Canada and the United States have dramatically different health care systems?

Figure **39** Starting a Business

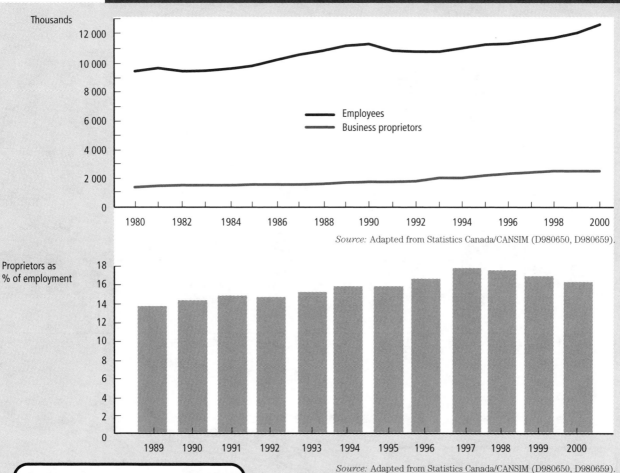

Net Number of Business Proprietors Compared to the Number of Employees

Thousands

Employees
Business proprietors

Source: Adapted from Statistics Canada/CANSIM (D980650, D980659).

Proprietors as % of employment

Source: Adapted from Statistics Canada/CANSIM (D980650, D980659).

The number of business proprietors, people who own their own **unincorporated businesses**, has risen as a proportion of total employment. As a proxy for entrepreneurial activity, this number is an understatement, since people who own their own **corporate enterprise** are excluded (they are counted as employees of their corporations). Proprietors of unincorporated businesses include those who employ others and those who employ only themselves. Some disparage self-employment as if it were of minor consequence, but all large enterprises begin small, and some start with just the founder. By exploring new business opportunities, entrepreneurs help society and its marketplaces **adapt to change**.

1. What caused the rapid increase in the number of entrepreneurs?

2. Why did the growth slow in the late 1990s?

3. What role has technology played in the growth of business proprietorship?

Figure 40 Who's Connected and Who's Not

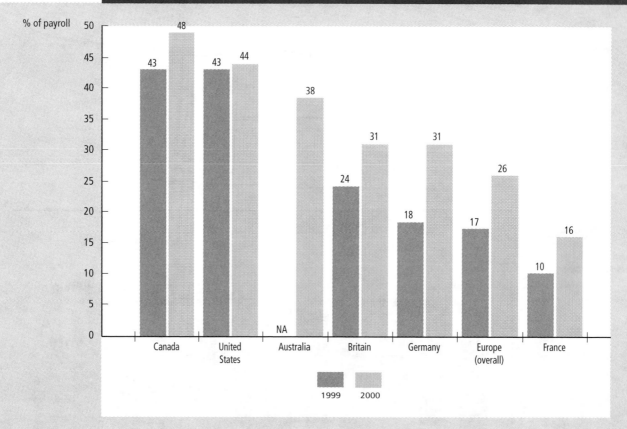

Percentage of Population Who Access the Internet at Home

% of payroll

Legend: 1999 | 2000

Canada: 43, 48
United States: 43, 44
Australia: NA, 38
Britain: 24, 31
Germany: 18, 31
Europe (overall): 17, 26
France: 10, 16

Source: PricewaterhouseCoopers, as reported in *The Globe and Mail*, 10 November 2000.

Notes: Respondents are those Internet users over 18 years of age.
NA = not available.

Some suggest that the rate at which the Internet is adopted serves as a proxy for a society's general **ability to adapt** to new technological possibilities. These people feel that the Internet is a vital technology that must be adopted and used aggressively, but there is considerable difference among countries with respect to their willingness to use new technologies.

1. Why do you think there is a difference between Canada and the United States in Internet use at home? Between Canada and the other countries?

2. Does Internet access at home reflect the ability of a country to adapt technologically? Or economically?

3. Is there a connection between Internet access at home and productivity growth?

Faster to Market

Number of Years between the Invention of a Technology and Its Use by 25 Percent of U.S. Households

Technology	Years between Invention and Use by 25 Percent of U.S. Households
Air conditioning	59
Telephone	39
Automobile	35
Radio	23
Personal computer	18
Cell phone	13
Internet access	7

Source: Adapted from Michael Cox, Federal Reserve Bank of Dallas, as reported in *Business Week*, 10 April 2000, p. 242.

The rate at which a new technology **diffuses** into the marketplace is a function of **competitive conditions**, the incentive to make a **profit**, and the strength of "**animal spirits**," among other factors. Technology itself is a source of competitive pressure. It serves society when technology diffuses quickly, thereby increasing consumer **utility**. Each new technology should be tested in the marketplace as quickly as possible to determine whether consumers see its value. Of course, consumers cannot signal their true intentions if the **private costs and benefits** of the technology do not match their **social costs and benefits**.

1. Why do recent innovations appear to enter the marketplace faster than did previous technologies?
2. How have competitive conditions changed since the invention of the telephone?
3. What role does the cost of the technology play in the speed of diffusion?
4. What is the role of "animal spirits," as described by John Maynard Keynes?

Figure 42 Ever Faster Competition

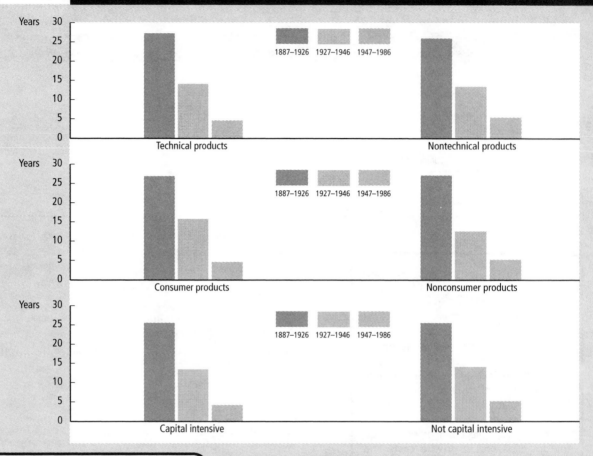

Average Number of Years between the Introduction of a New Product and the Arrival of Competitors

1887–1926   1927–1946   1947–1986

Technical products   Nontechnical products

Consumer products   Nonconsumer products

Capital intensive   Not capital intensive

Source: Rajashree Agarwal and Michael Gort, "First-Mover Advantage and the Speed of Competitive Entry, 1986–1987, *Journal of Law and Economics*, April 2001, reported in *Economic Intuition*, Spring 2001, p. 25.

One indication of **competitive** pressure is the average number of years between the introduction of a new product and the arrival in the marketplace of competitors offering the same product. In other words, this measures the number of years in which the original innovator has an **effective monopoly**. This monopolistic edge has been declining over the past century and competitors now arrive in the marketplace faster, which limits the duration of the **monopoly profit** available from innovation. Clearly, the **barriers to entry** must be falling and the **diffusion of skill and knowledge** rising. It does not appear to matter whether the product is technically based, is a consumer product, or is capital intensive.

1. Why are the barriers to entry falling? Which particular barriers are falling?

2. Why are technological products in the same apparent situation as consumer products?

3. When the research is completed for the period after 1986, are there reasons to expect technological products will face different competitive conditions than consumer products?

4. Would you expect the trend toward faster competition to continue?

Part III: Financial Markets

The financial markets facilitate the transfer of money and financial assets and by doing so provide the "lubrication" for all marketplace transactions. Since our society is now far too complex for widespread barter exchange, the prosperity of the "real" economy rests on the platform of a secure, smoothly functioning financial system. Some markets trade shares of ownership (equity) and others trade debt (bond and money markets).

This part includes discussion of

- Stock Markets
- Interest Rates
- Average Prices
- Balance Sheet
- Public Finances

Figure 43 The Real and the Virtual

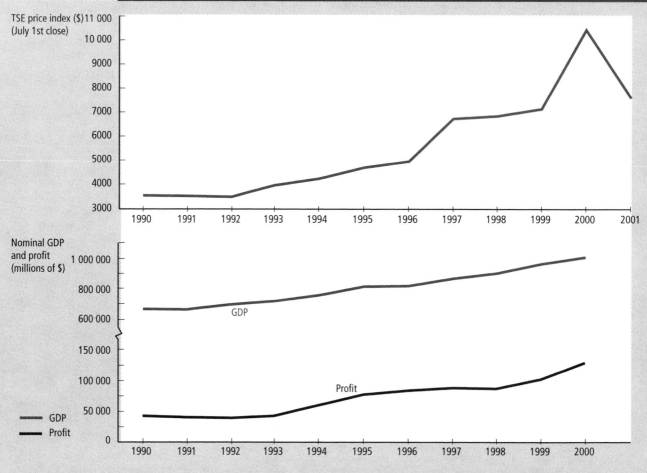

The Toronto Stock Exchange: Price Index and Nominal GDP/Profit

Source: Adapted from Statistics Canada/CANSIM (Matrix 6521);
<http://ca.finance.yahoo.com>.

The prices on the Toronto Stock Exchange (TSE) reflect investors' expectations about the companies listed on the exchange. These **publicly traded companies** are strongly affected by the state of the **overall economy**, as measured by **GDP**. In particular, as the pace of the economy grows or slows, so, too, should the pace of **corporate profit**. This correlation is true even though many corporations are not publicly traded.

1. How close is the connection between the TSE price index and GDP? Between the TSE price index and corporate profits?

2. *Should* each relationship be closer? Are there lags?

3. Why is the connection with nominal, instead of real, GDP or profit?

Figure **44** The Great Tech Crash

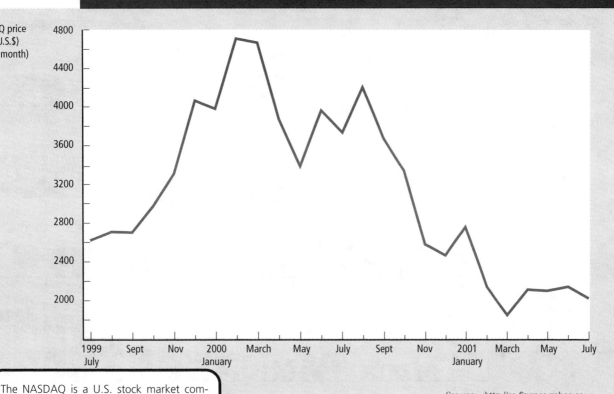

The NASDAQ Stock Price Index Close, End of the Month

NASDAQ price index (U.S.$) (end of month)

Source: <http://ca.finance.yahoo.ca>.

The NASDAQ is a U.S. stock market comprising primarily technology companies, and it is often used as a benchmark for the general state of the U.S. **technology sector**. It is particularly important to this sector since technology companies frequently issue stock (**raise equity capital**) to fuel growth. In the 1990s the NASDAQ rose very rapidly. Between 17 July 1995 and 3 November 1999, the index increased by 2000 points, but this rate of growth was plainly **unsustainable**. The sector's output and **profits** were rising much more slowly, and the overall U.S. economy was growing by single digits. The market had become irrational, responding to its own momentum, and oblivious to economic reality. Start-up companies rushed to raise equity, and "dot-coms" blossomed, many of them without marketing or strategic plans. The telecommunications companies rushed to build capacity. The NASDAQ peaked near 5000, and then the bubble burst. Billions of dollars of investor value were lost, **capital for technology** vanished, and the technology sector slowed severely.

1. What did investors need to know to avoid taking large losses as the NASDAQ tumbled? Was the information available?
2. What particular circumstances broke the "bubble"? Were those circumstances predictable?
3. Have there been similar stock market excesses in the past? When do you think there will be another one?

Figure 45 What Makes the Market Move?

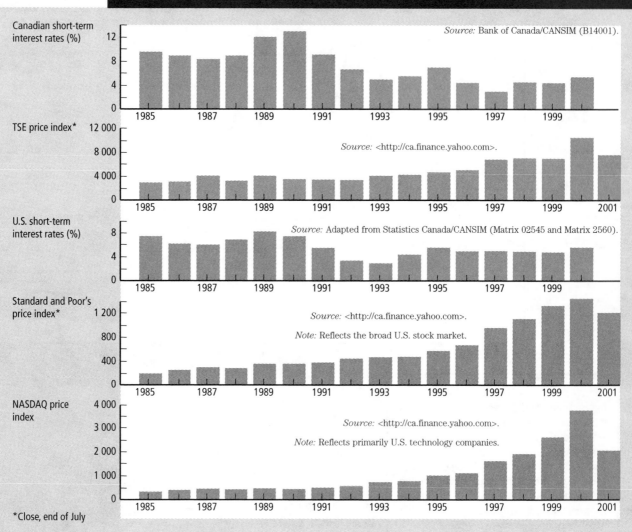

Interest Rates and the North American Stock Markets

Canadian short-term interest rates (%)

Source: Bank of Canada/CANSIM (B14001).

TSE price index*

Source: <http://ca.finance.yahoo.com>.

U.S. short-term interest rates (%)

Source: Adapted from Statistics Canada/CANSIM (Matrix 02545 and Matrix 2560).

Standard and Poor's price index*

Source: <http://ca.finance.yahoo.com>.

Note: Reflects the broad U.S. stock market.

NASDAQ price index

Source: <http://ca.finance.yahoo.com>.

Note: Reflects primarily U.S. technology companies.

*Close, end of July

The stock markets behave in broadly predictable ways, as do all economic variables. However, the stock market in particular exhibits an occasional, temporary lack of connection to underlying economic variables. A company's stock is ultimately valuable only in relation to the **profit** that company can generate. The market will buy and the stock price will rise in **expectation of future profit**. But when interest rates rise, the economy slows, and when the economy slows, profits decrease. As a result, stock prices are likely also to fall.

1. Why did the stock market price declines of 2000–01 surprise so many investors?

2. Why was the technology sector not immune from this decline in value?

3. Why were NASDAQ prices more severely affected than those in Standard and Poor's index?

4. How do the Canadian and U.S. stock markets affect each other?

5. In what ways have the decline in stock market values affected individual welfare and the overall economy?

Figure **46** What Makes Interest Rates Go Up or Down?

The Money Supply (M1) and Interest Rates

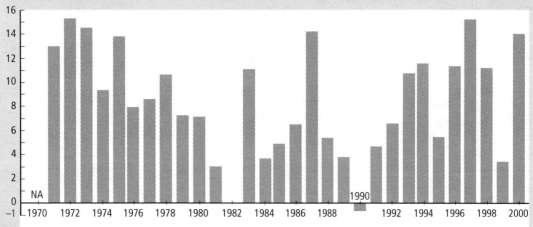

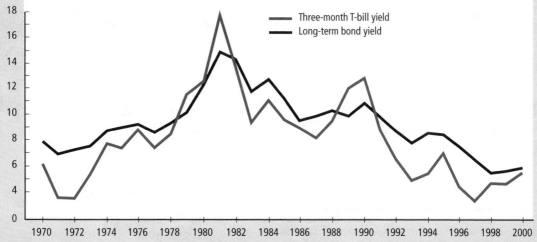

Source: Bank of Canada/CANSIM (B2033).

Note: Long-term bond yields are the average yield on government bonds with 10 or more years to maturity.

Monetary policy affects both the **money supply (monetary aggregates)** and interest rates. There are two kinds of interest rates: those for **short-term** and **long-term** credit. Each rate has a different effect on economic activity, and, of course, they affect the rate of **GDP growth**.

1. Why are interest rates affected by the money supply? Are there other factors involved?

2. Why are short-term and long-term rates different? Why does the *spread* between these two rates widen or narrow?

3. What caused the increase in interest rates in the early 1980s and the early 1990s? Why are interest rates much lower now?

4. What causes the M1 money supply to rise at different rates?

Figure 47 How Much Did That Loan Really Cost?

Real Interest Rates

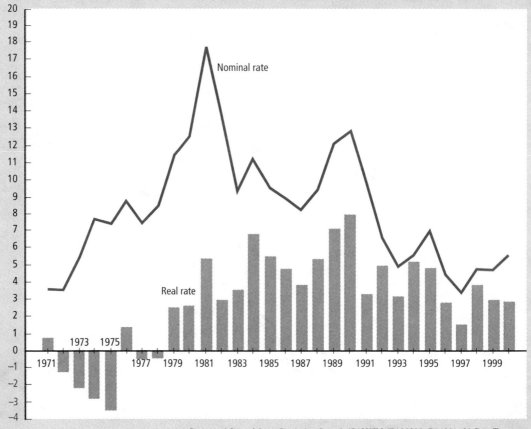

Source: Adapted from Statistics Canada/CANSIM (P100000, B14001: 91-Day Treasury Bill Tender).

Note: The real rates are deflated by the changes in Consumer Price Index.

When one person or organization borrows money from another, the interest rate is the reward that goes to the lender. For the borrower, the interest rate is the cost of the loan. Both parties need to know the **true reward** and **cost** of the transaction to make an informed decision. The rate of inflation alters the interest rate, because loans exist over **time** and the interest payments are made over time. The price level also changes over time and, therefore, the **purchasing power** of a set amount of money changes. As the **price level** rises, the purchasing power of the same amount of money falls. Since a lender wants the loan to return an increase in purchasing power, the **real rate of interest** must be calculated. This is the nominal (stated) rate less the rate of inflation.

1. If the real rate of inflation is negative, who benefits? The lender or the borrower?

2. If inflation is difficult to predict, why would a lender not want to lend money at a fixed interest rate fixed for a long period?

3. What is the economic effect when borrowers cannot borrow money at fixed rates for long periods?

Figure 48

Cheaper to Borrow in Canada or the United States?

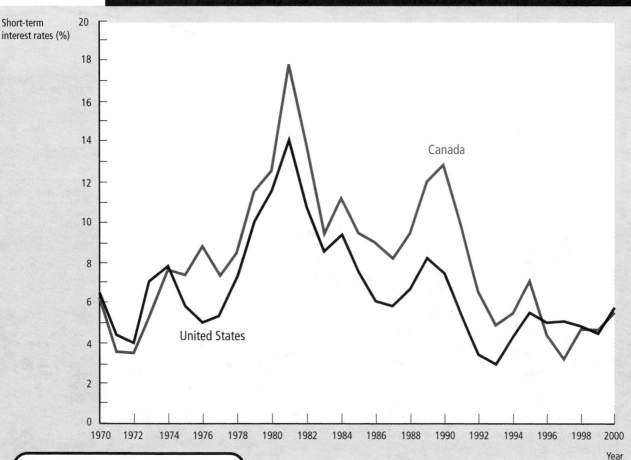

Canadian and U.S. Short-Term Interest Rates

Short-term interest rates (%)

Canada

United States

Year

Source: Adapted from Statistics Canada/CANSIM (Matrix 02545; B14001, B54401).

Canada and the United States have followed broadly similar **monetary policies**. Both countries forced interest rates higher in the early 1980s and 1990s, and in the mid-1990s, in response to concerns about rising **inflation**. For much of this period, interest rates in Canada were higher than in the United States, discouraging **borrowing** in Canada. The gap later closed and since 1996, Canada's rates have usually been below or close to the U.S. rate. As a result, borrowing in Canada is available on terms close to those in the United States.

1. Why is it helpful to the Canadian economy to have Canadian interest rates similar to those in the United States?

2. Have long-term interest rates in Canada and the United States also converged?

3. Why did Canadian and U.S. interest rates rise in 2000?

Figure **49** Inflation: The Great Enemy

The Consumer Price Index and Inflation

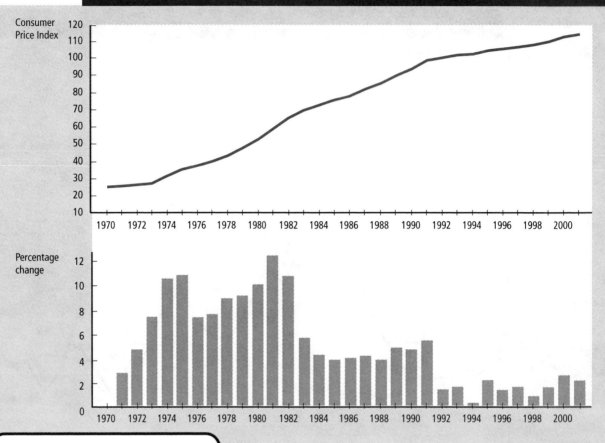

Source: Adapted from Statistics Canada/CANSIM (P100000).

Inflation is the rate at which *average* prices rise. Although individual prices may fall, the level of average prices normally rises. Inflation is measured in several ways, but the most common is based on the Consumer Price Index (CPI). This index measures the average price for a bundle of goods and services typically purchased by households, but excludes the price of items like industrial machinery, for example. Consumer inflation, therefore, measures the *rate* at which the CPI rises. Rising inflation has long been a concern of **public policy**, and **monetary** and **fiscal policy** have been used to control or moderate inflation. High inflation can destabilize the financial system, distort the allocation of resources, and redistribute income inequitably. Rising inflation also suggests that the economy is approaching its output capacity and that the present course of the economy is unsustainable.

1. Characterize the long-term trend of the rate of inflation.
2. How did public policy successful restrain inflation?
3. What public policy tools were used to reduce inflation?
4. What costs were involved in reducing inflation?

Figure **The Financial Duo**

Interest Rates and Inflation

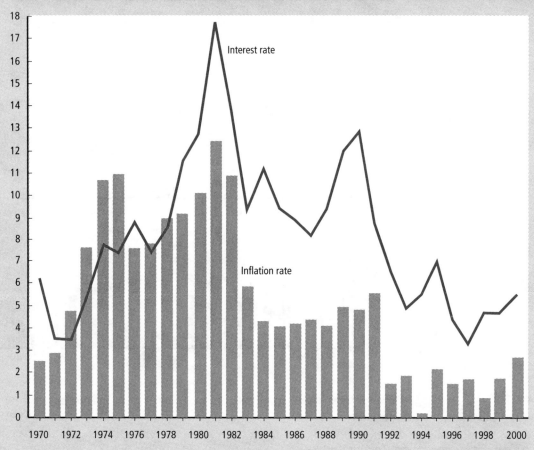

Interest and inflation rates (%)

Source: Adapted from Statistics Canada/CANSIM (P100000; B14001)

Note: Interest rates are measured here by 91-day Treasury bills. Inflation is measured by the CPI.

Interest rates and inflation are both key variables in the **financial markets**, and both play important roles in the operation of the **macroeconomy**. The Bank of Canada uses interest rates as a **monetary policy tool** whose goal is to restrain inflation. The application of restrictive, anti-inflationary policy usually causes interest rates to rise and inflation to fall. Unfortunately, this effect comes with a slowdown in **economic activity** and **employment** levels.

1. What groups in society benefit from rising interest rates?
2. In what way do anti-inflationary policies redistribute income?
3. How do Canada's monetary policies compare to those of the United States?

Figure 51

The Power of Interest Rates

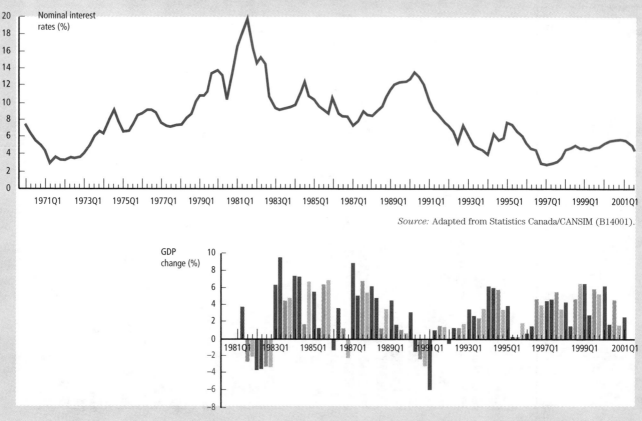

Interest Rates and Real GDP by Quarterly Change

Source: Adapted from Statistics Canada/CANSIM (B14001).

Source: Adapted from Statistics Canada/CANSIM (Matrix 2560; D100151).

Interest rates have a powerful effect on overall economic activity. When interest rates rise significantly, it becomes more expensive to finance purchases and more **expensive for businesses to borrow to invest in plant, machinery, and equipment**. Rising interest rates slow the economy, and if they rise enough, a **recession** (two consecutive quarters of contraction) follows. Thus, the two most recent recessions (1981–82, and 1990–91) and the **economic slowdown** in the mid-1990s were not surprising. Nor was the fact that interest rates were rising; their increase was the intended effect of **monetary policy** conducted by the **Bank of Canada**.

1. Why do many people and businesses seem surprised when the economy slows because of monetary policy?

2. How does an economic slowdown affect labour markets and the stock markets?

3. What *other* factors affect the rate of growth of the economy?

4. How could an individual or business prepare for economic slowdown?

Figure 52 Which Leads Which?

Inflation and Wage Settlements

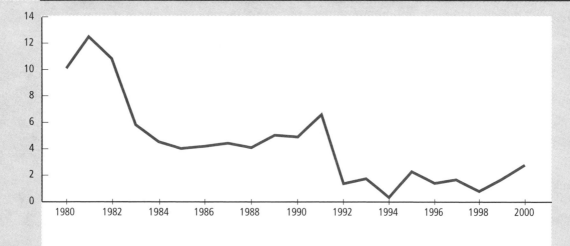

Inflation rate (%)

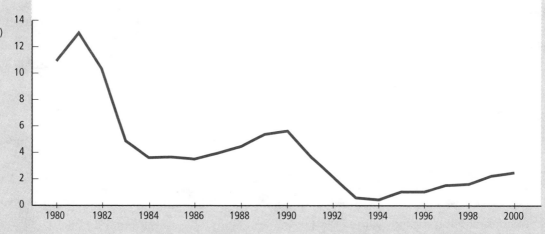

Wage settlement rate of change (%)

Source: Adapted from Statistics Canada/CANSIM (P100000) and *Perspectives on Labour and Income*, Autumn 2000, Vol. 12, no. 3, "Unionization—An Update." Available at <http://www.statcan.ca/english/indepth/75-001/feature/pehi2000012003s3a94.htm>.

A very close relationship exists between inflation, measured by the Consumer Price Index (CPI), and the rate of increase of wage settlements. Both are strongly driven by **macroeconomic conditions**, but the CPI appears to be more sensitive to changes in **aggregate demand**, reflected in GDP growth, and wage settlements seem to be more closely linked to **conditions in the labour markets**. Debate continues about whether inflation is driven by wage settlements or vice versa. In the past, it is clear that workers negotiated their wage settlements in light of what they thought inflation might be (**expected inflation**). Inflation and wage settlements are best seen as mutually interdependent.

1. What caused inflation *and* wage rates to fall sharply in 1983?
2. What were labour market conditions like in 1983?
3. What were the aggregate demand conditions like between 1980 and 1983?
4. How sensitive are workers today to inflation? Why has their sensitivity changed?

Figure  Wealth According to Accountants

National Balance Sheet

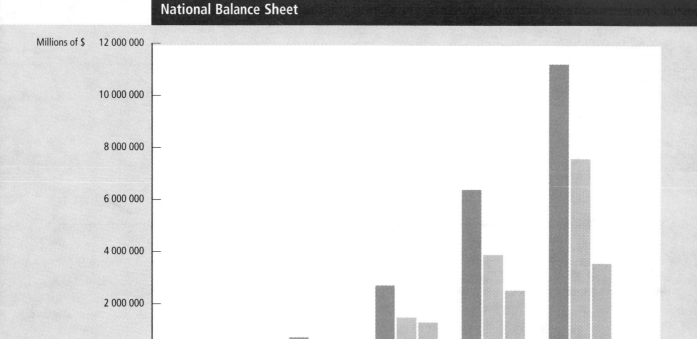

Millions of $

Source: Adapted from Statistics Canada/CANSIM (Matrices 0751, 0753, 0757, 0761, 0768, 0772, 0776, 0779, 0782, 0790).

Economic and financial circumstances are measured in many ways. Balance sheets using standard accounting conventions are a common business tool, and they can be applied to an entire country. **Assets** measure the value of what is owned, and **liabilities** measure what is owed. Positive net worth reflects the amount by which assets exceed the value of liabilities, and it is considered a sign of financial prudence. For Canada, net worth has been rising, so by this calculation, national wealth has been increasing. Wealth, of course, is different from actual income that is available for spending.

1. How does national net worth relate to GDP growth?

2. Why is it not possible to understand the consequences of liabilities without knowing the level of assets?

3. How does the rate of inflation affect net worth?

Figure 54

How Much Wealth Is There to Go Around?

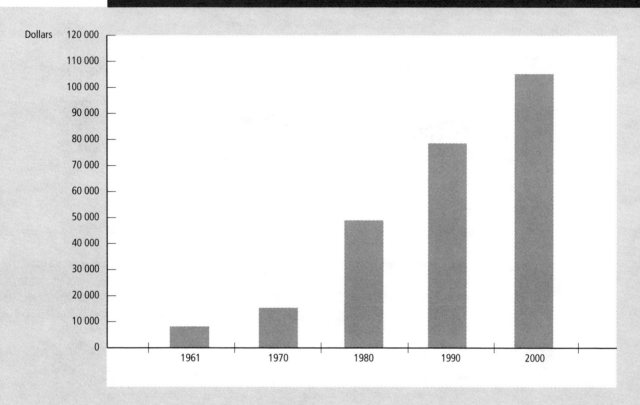

Net Worth per Person

Source: Adapted from Statistics Canada/CANSIM (D1; Matrices 0751, 0753, 0757, 0761, 0768, 0772, 0776, 0779, 0782, 0790).

It is important to measure net worth on a per person basis, as with GDP. This value is affected by a wide range of influences, including the rate of growth of the population, the state of the **financial markets**, and the level of **real output**. Many people do pay close attention to their personal or family net worth, using it as an indication of their wealth to help them plan their financial future.

1. Why did net worth change so dramatically from 1961 to 2000?

2. What happened to GDP per person during the same period?

3. In what way does net worth affect consumer and investor confidence? Why is economic confidence important?

Figure

Who Has the Most Wealth?

Balance Sheet: Positive Net Worth, 2000

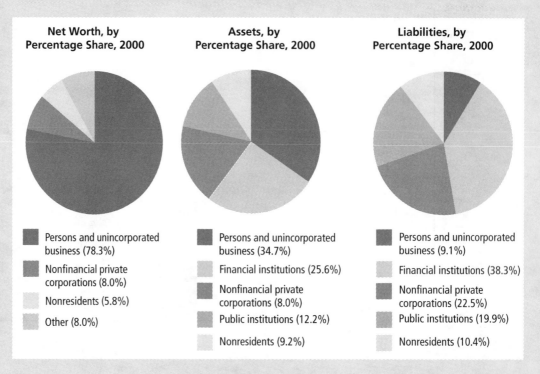

Net Worth, by Percentage Share, 2000

- Persons and unincorporated business (78.3%)
- Nonfinancial private corporations (8.0%)
- Nonresidents (5.8%)
- Other (8.0%)

Assets, by Percentage Share, 2000

- Persons and unincorporated business (34.7%)
- Financial institutions (25.6%)
- Nonfinancial private corporations (8.0%)
- Public institutions (12.2%)
- Nonresidents (9.2%)

Liabilities, by Percentage Share, 2000

- Persons and unincorporated business (9.1%)
- Financial institutions (38.3%)
- Nonfinancial private corporations (22.5%)
- Public institutions (19.9%)
- Nonresidents (10.4%)

Source: Adapted from Statistics Canada/CANSIM (Matrices 0751, 0753, 0757, 0761, 0768, 0772, 0776, 0779, 0782, 0790).

Notes: Amounts may not sum to 100 percent because of rounding. Net worth excludes sectors with negative net worth.

By some standards, corporations have great wealth and power. But to understand any issue, it is helpful to view it from **different perspectives**. Although corporations hold high levels of assets, these are set against heavy liabilities. Individuals and unincorporated businesses hold even greater assets and their liabilities are much smaller. The result is a disproportionate share of net worth held largely by individuals and unincorporated enterprises.

1. Why do persons and unincorporated businesses have relatively low liabilities compared with nonfinancial corporations?
2. Why do corporations, by contrast, have much higher liabilities?
3. In what forms do individuals and unincorporated businesses hold their assets?

Figure **56** What the Public Sector Owns and Owes

Public Institutions: Balance Sheet, 2000

	Assets	Liabilities	Net Worth
	(Millions of $)		
Federal government	145 771	633 605	(487 834)
Monetary authorities	85 601	85 094	507
Public financial institutions	102 580	93 867	8 713
Social security funds	60 488	0	60 488
Nonfinancial government enterprises	268 406	178 302	90 104
Other government and hospitals	696 864	533 798	163 066

Source: Adapted from Statistics Canada/CANSIM (Matrices 0751, 0753, 0757, 0761, 0768, 0772, 0776, 0779, 0782, 0790)

The public is rightly concerned about the **financial prudence** of its governmental agencies, since the federal government carries a high negative net worth. However, the issue must be interpreted carefully. First, some parts of the federal government's assets are not included—the value of natural resources on federal Crown lands, for example. The values are excluded because they are too speculative. Second, other levels of government have spending mandates that inherently create asset value on a traditional balance sheet. By contrast, part of federal spending is directed to activities that create **intangible value** that will not appear on a traditional balance sheet, such as the value of scientific discoveries funded by the agencies that support university research.

1. Is the federal financial situation improving or deteriorating?
2. What kinds of provincial and municipal spending naturally create asset value?
3. Why do the monetary authorities have their assets almost equal to their liabilities?

Figure

Federal Finances: Under Control

Budgetary Position of the Government of Canada, Fiscal 2000

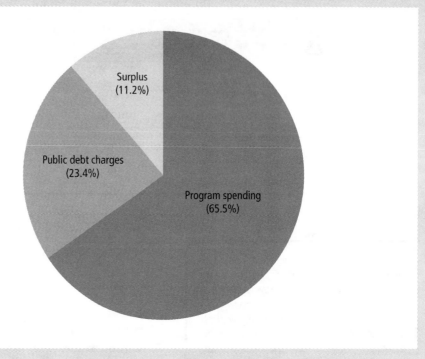

Source: Adapted from Statistics Canada/CANSIM (Matrix 0154; Matrix 0151).

Leaving behind their long-run budgetary **deficit** (where spending exceeds revenues), the federal government is now running a **surplus**. The surplus is being used to reduce the absolute amount of the **public debt**. However, **public debt charges** (interest that is paid on the outstanding debt) continue to take a significant share of tax revenues. This share will fall over time as the debt itself does. The shift from deficit to surplus is the result of reduced spending as a percentage of GDP, a moderate increase in the effective tax rate, and sustained economic growth.

1. Why did it take the government so long to move from a deficit to a surplus position?

2. Why did the government run its previous deficits?

3. Should the government continue to run a surplus to pay down the debt? Or should it lower taxes? Or should it do both?

Figure **58** The Disappearing Deficit

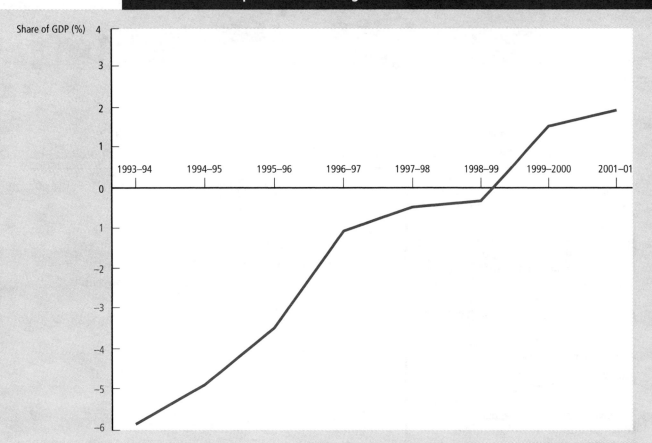

Federal Deficit/Surplus as a Percentage of GDP

Source: *Budget Papers, Ministry of Finance 1993–2000*; adapted from Statistics Canada/CANSIM (Matrix 0151; D14840).

Measuring the deficit as a percentage of GDP shows the speed with which the deficit was eliminated. At more than 5 percent of GDP in fiscal 1993–94, federal borrowing was very high and the **net debt** was growing at an **unsustainable** rate. The situation had arisen because of previous decisions, some taken many years ago. Part of the difficulty was that the public generally is in favour of spending but not tax increases. In a democratic state like Canada, the ultimate responsibility for the appropriateness of **public finances** rests with the people.

1. Does the public take its responsibility for government finances seriously enough?

2. Does the public take the time to understand the state of government finances?

3. Why does the Canadian public seem so pessimistic about any economic challenge facing the country? (And then sometimes fail to notice it has been solved?)

Figure 59

A Bad Year, A Good Year

Federal Budget Summary, Fiscal 1993 and 1997

	1993–94	1997–98
	(Billions of $)	
Budgetary revenues	116.0	153.2
Program spending	−120.0	−108.8
Operating balance	−4.0	44.4
Public debt charges	−38.0	−40.9
Budget balance	−42.0	3.5

Source: Budget Papers 1996 and 2000, Ministry of Finance, Canada.

Fiscal 1993 and 1997 are a study in contrasts. In 1993 the government's revenues could not even cover **program spending**. The **operating balance** was in deficit and that sum ($4.0 billion) had to be borrowed, along with the interest due on the **net debt** ($38.0 billion). In other words, the government added new debt to cover the interest payments on its old debt and borrowed more to meet program needs. By 1997, the situation had greatly changed. Program spending had fallen and tax revenues were up because of tax increases and economic growth. These changes produced an operating balance of $44.4 billion, *more* than enough to cover the debt charges (interest payments) of $40.9 billion. A government surplus resulted. The credit for the turnaround belongs to Canadians, who accepted the need for tax increases and spending cuts and worked to increase the output of the economy.

1. What types of spending did the government reduce?
2. What taxes were increased?
3. What role did monetary policy play in this turnaround?

Figure 60 Fiscal Freedom

Saving and Borrowing, 1993 and 1997

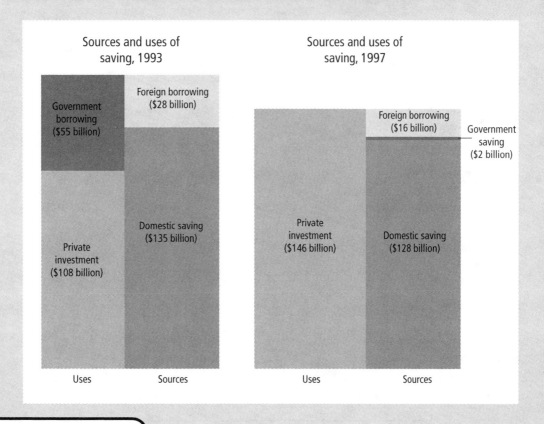

Source: *Budget Papers 1998*, Ministry of Finance, Canada.

The danger involved in government borrowing is that it may "**crowd out**" private investment. When private investment decreases, the future productive capacity of the economy is less than it could have been. This effect arises because government borrowing uses up some of the domestic savings that would otherwise be available to private investment. Moreover, if public borrowing and private investment exceed domestic saving, Canada must borrow from foreign sources, leaving Canada vulnerable to the conditions and opinions of the foreign lenders. In 1993, foreign borrowing ($28 billion) was necessary to meet the needs of government and the private sector. By 1997, investment had risen and all levels of government combined were net savers, in effect supporting private investment. Foreign borrowing had fallen and also directly supported private investment.

1. How do foreigners decide whether to invest in either public bonds or private Canadian investment?
2. What other factors contributed to this shift in borrowing?
3. In what way does this shift in borrowing contribute to Canada's long-term rate of growth?
4. What social disadvantages might be reflected in the achievement of these numbers?

Figure **61** How Big a Bite?

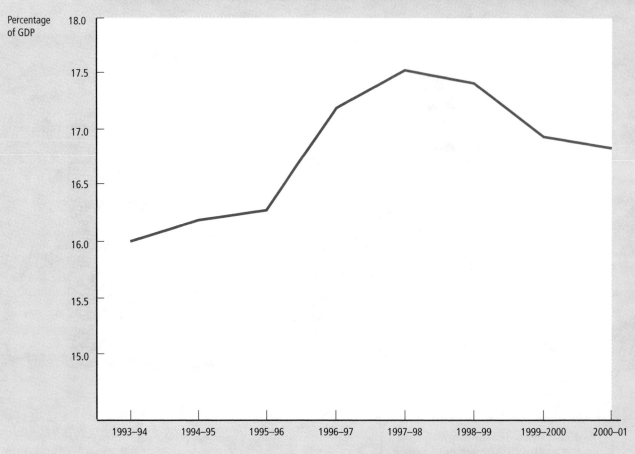

Federal Tax Revenues as a Percentage of GDP

Percentage of GDP

Source: Budget Papers 1993–2000, Ministry of Finance; Adapted from Statistics Canada/CANSIM (Matrix 0151; D14840).

The **effective federal tax rate** rose to help reduce the deficit between fiscal 1993 and fiscal 1997. An approximate increase in GDP of 1.5 percentage points over this period is clearly significant, since it is an almost 10 percent increase in the *rate*. Because the federal government was facing a **structural deficit** (built in by the basic pattern of its spending and taxation policies), rebalancing the tax rate was the logical tool to use. Whether the federal government should have used another tool to reduce the deficit, or used tax increases to a lesser or greater degree, is a matter of public debate. Part of the tax increase has now been reversed.

1. What did the electoral choices of Canadians during this period suggest about the acceptability of these tax increases?
2. What factors may cause tax rates to be further reduced?
3. Why must tax increases be judged in the overall context of government spending and social priorities?

Figure **What Kinds of Taxes?**

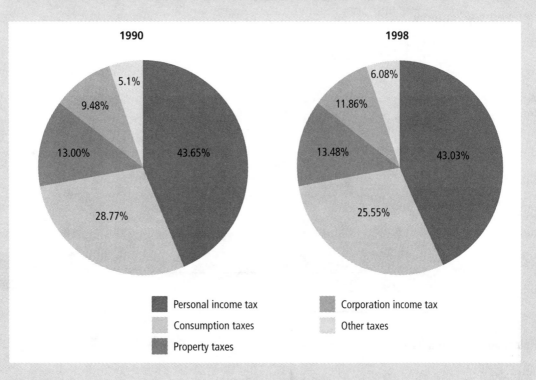

Tax Categories: All Governments by Share of Total Tax

1990

5.1%
9.48%
13.00%
28.77%
43.65%

1998

6.08%
11.86%
13.48%
25.55%
43.03%

■ Personal income tax ■ Corporation income tax

■ Consumption taxes ■ Other taxes

■ Property taxes

Source: Adapted from Statistics Canada/CANSIM (Matrix 03317).

The governments of Canada have a clear preference for **income taxes**. Other countries, like the United States, rely less on income taxes. The **relative shares** of various categories of taxes have not varied significantly over the past decade, excluding a modest increase in corporate tax and an approximately equivalent decline in consumption taxes. **Consumption taxes**, including sales taxes and the GST, represent the second largest share of total taxes. Income taxes are considered more **socially equitable** than consumption taxes; however, measures can be used to make consumption taxes more equitable. Since the federal government and some provincial governments are lowering income taxes, the income tax proportion is now falling.

1. What kind of incentive effects do different kinds of taxes have on economic activity?

2. Do the incentive effects of taxes tend to conflict with considerations of social equity?

3. How can a society balance the encouragement of economic growth with the objective of social equity?

The Weight of Federal Spending

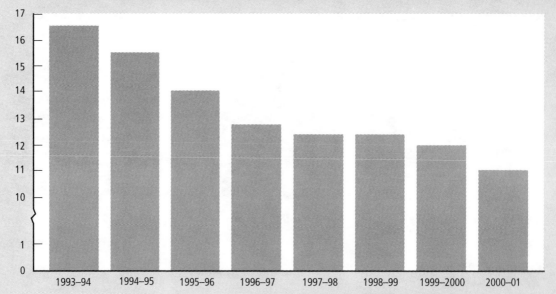

Program Spending as a Percentage of GDP

Source: *Budget Papers 1993–2000*, Ministry of Finance; adapted from Statistics Canada/CANSIM (Matrix 0151; D14840).

When the public wants to hold the **government accountable** for its spending decisions, the focus must be on program spending. This Figure includes all public spending, except **public debt charges** (interest on the national debt). Since interest must be paid on the amount already borrowed, the government cannot affect this amount. Thus, they should be held responsible for what they can control now: program spending. Contrary to popular opinion, program spending has been reduced sharply as a percentage of GDP. Since the burden of spending is measured by its impact on the total **spending and resources** of an economy, it must be related to GDP. Program spending reached a postwar peak of over 19 percent in mid-1970s, and by the early 1980s was again rapidly approaching that level. By the mid-1980s the government began reducing program spending in real terms. Program spending rose briefly in the early 1990s as **automatic stabilizers** were engaged by the recession, then it continued its decline. By the beginning of the 2000s, all the postwar increase in program spending had been reversed and spending stood at close to the amount in 1950.

1. Why do many people believe that federal spending remains high?

2. Is spending high by some other standard? Are other standards appropriate?

3. What effects have there been of this sustained and significant reduction in public spending by the Government of Canada?

Figure **64** The Tax Burden in the G7 Countries

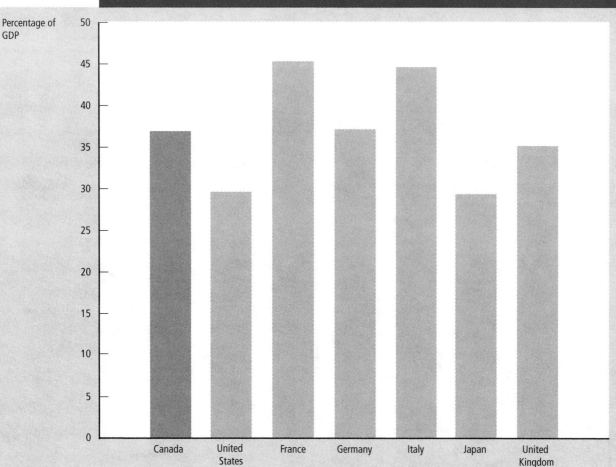

Total Tax Receipts as a Percentage of GDP, 1997

Percentage of GDP

Source: Organisation for Economic Co-operation and Development (OECD),
OECD in Figures 2000, <www.oecd.org>.

Total taxes as a percentage of GDP vary considerably among major countries: Japan and United States have the lowest effective tax rates; Canada's rate is in the mid-range. (Note that tax reductions made since 1997 may have caused this rate to fall in Canada.) Although taxes as a percentage of GDP are an important indicator, they represent only half the **economic equation**. Tax rates by themselves cannot be judged as appropriate or not; they must be compared to the benefits of taxation, that is, to the **public services** and **transfer payments** they provide. Unfortunately, the values of these public services are difficult to judge, since they have different value to different people. Some, for example, view environmental protection as having high value; others see it as having lesser value.

1. Why does the comparison between Canadian and U.S. tax rates have more potential impact than the comparison with European rates?

2. Are there differences between Canada and the United States to account for the differences in the tax rates?

3. What public services do Canadian governments provide? How valuable are they to you?

Figure 65 How Heavy Is the Debt?

Federal Net Debt as a Percentage of GDP

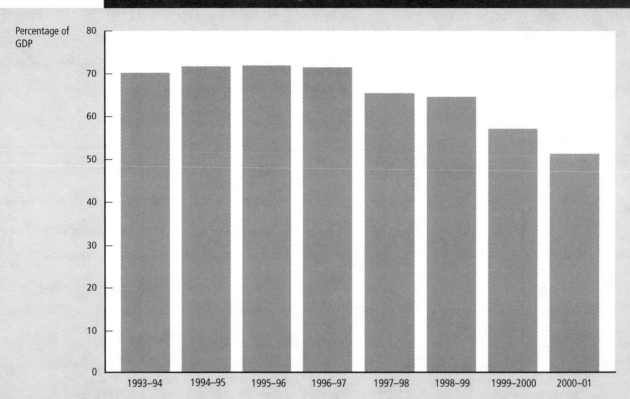

Percentage of GDP

Source: Budget Papers 1993–2000, Ministry of Finance; adapted from Statistics Canada/CANSIM (Matrix 0151; D14840).

As with **program spending**, net public debt must be measured as a percentage of GDP. The burden of debt on the capital (credit) markets is a function of the size of the debt, compared with the size of the **financial capital pools**. Those pools grow as the economy grows. This percentage is much more significant than whether the debt grows or shrinks as an absolute number. The debt's percentage of GDP hit a record high of over 100 percent of GDP at the end of World War II, with government's massive military spending. The debt then declined rapidly, reaching a low point in the mid-1970s, at under 20 percent of GDP. The debt ratio rose from there, and started to fall again in the late 1990s.

1. Why are the size of GDP and a country's capital pools so important to understanding the burden of the public debt?

2. Why did the debt ratio rise after the mid-1970s? Why did it rise for so long?

3. Why could the debt ratio still fall even if there still were a deficit?

Part IV: Individual Success

Individual success requires a range of economic responses. With the support of family, the individual must choose both a career and an employer. The resulting household income must be spent wisely to ensure it is contributing to welfare, not waste. Finally, most households want to commit some of their resources to investments that will provide a source of nonemployment income. To make these decisions effectively, the individual must apply both macroeconomic and microeconomic principles. Of particular importance are the state of the labour markets and the income flows they generate.

This part includes discussion of

- Employment
- Productivity and Wages
- Standard of Living

Figure 66 The Job Engine

Employment and the Growth Rate of Real GDP

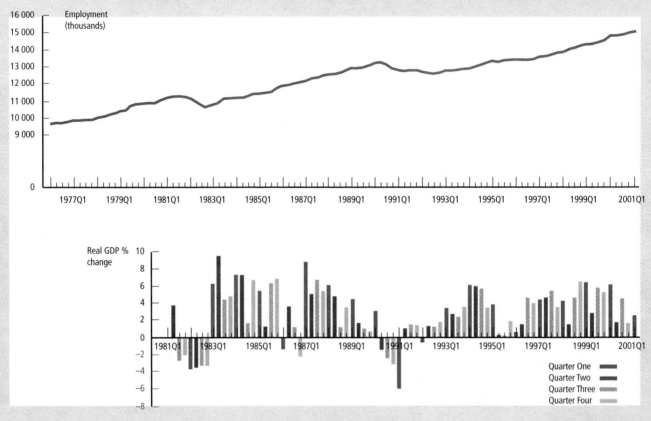

Source: Statistics Canada and adapted from Statistics Canada/CANSIM (D980595, D100151).

As the economy grows (measured by rate of **real GDP** growth) employment normally rises, but only when the economy grows faster than the rate of increase of output per worker (productivity). Thus the economy can grow (at the same rate of productivity) without adding workers. Fortunately, it usually grows faster and needs to add workers, but when **aggregate demand** weakens, both **output** and **employment** slow. Therefore, a direct relationship exists between the determinants of aggregate demand and employment.

1. Why did employment levels fall in 1981–82 and 1991–92? Why did they barely increase in 1995?
2. Why were these slowdowns predictable?
3. Why does employment usually increase?
4. What is the normal range for productivity growth?

Figure **67** How Many Working? How Many Not?

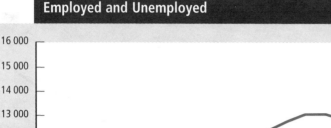

Employed and Unemployed

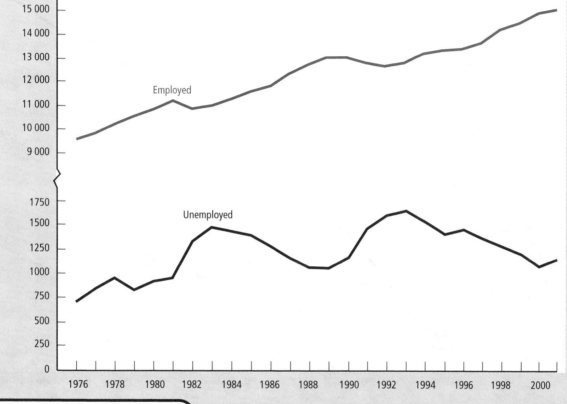

Number (thousands)

Source: Adapted from Statistics Canada/CANSIM (D980595, D980712).

Employed Canadians are the economy's **principal resource**, and a rising level of employment reflects **economic prosperity** both collectively and individually. Unemployed Canadians (people who want to work and cannot find work) represent a waste of talent and energy. Both employment growth and unemployment are affected by the **aggregate demand** conditions that drive **GDP growth**. However, unemployment is also affected by the growth in the working-age population *and* the people's desire to work (the **participation rate**). Some people of working age choose not to work in the paid labour force. They may choose to attend to home or family responsibilities, retire, or attend school, pursuits not directly affected by the economy. Thus, although employment growth is a direct indication of the pace of economic activity, unemployment is affected by both social and economic concerns.

1. Why do employment and unemployment rise at different rates? Why do they sometimes move in opposite directions?

2. If employment falls by 1000, why will unemployment not automatically rise by the same amount?

3. What is the "normal" trend for Canadian employment?

Figure 68 Good Jobs or Poor Jobs, 1976–2000

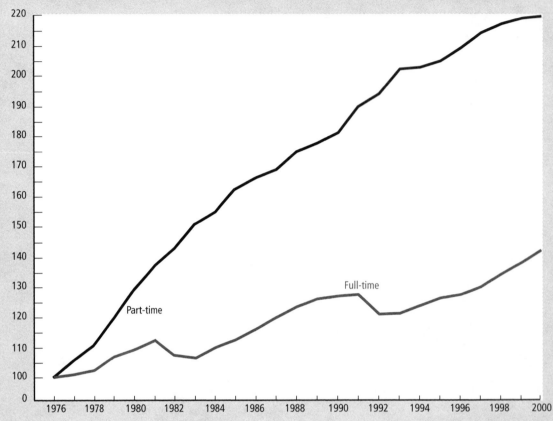

Rate of Employment Change

Rate of change in employment 1976 = 100

Part-time

Full-time

Source: Adapted from Statistics Canada/CANSIM (D980699, D980686).

Notes: Shows the rate of change, not the number working.
Full-time and part-time workers in 1976 set at 100.

Most people want more than just a job; they want a good income with reasonable security and opportunities for advancement. Many people believe that all part-time jobs are, therefore, undesirable and that they are the result of weak **economic growth** and inappropriate **public policies**.

1. Why has part-time employment risen faster than full-time employment for so long?

2. Is this a sign of economic distress? Partly or fully?

3. What other characteristics define good or poor jobs?

Figure 69

Part-Timers: Luxury of Choice?

Part-Time Workers as a Percentage of Total Workers, and Voluntary and Involuntary Part-Time Workers as a Percentage of Total Part-Time Workers

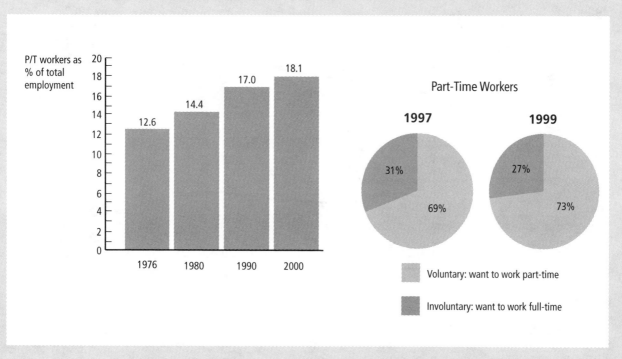

Source: Statistics Canada/*Perspectives*, November 2000 (75-001-XIE).

Employment **choices**, like all economic choices, involve individual **preferences** arising from differing **utility functions**. It is thus unwise to attribute one person's preferences to another person. Of course, these choices are always made in light of overall **macroeconomic conditions**.

1. Who tends to work part time?
2. Why do some people choose to work part time? Because of another wage earner in the family? As a reflection of general affluence?

Figure 70 Surging Service Employment

Employment in the Goods and Services Sectors

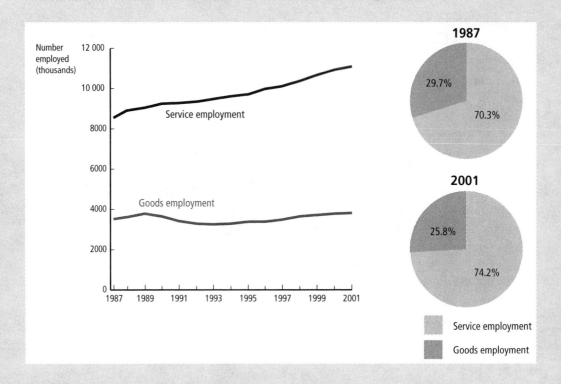

Source: Direct and adapted from Statistics Canada/CANSIM (D968123, D968117).

The service orientation of the economy is clearly shown in the differences between the growth of employment in the service and goods sectors. This growth is driven partly by **customer preferences** and partly by **technological constraints**. Considerable debate exists about the quality of jobs in the goods sector compared to the service sector. Manufacturing jobs often pay high wages, and service jobs, such as in restaurants, pay low wages. But manufacturing also includes smaller operations that pay more modest wages, and the service sector includes computing consultants who are generally very well paid.

1. Has the growth of service sector employment affected the differences in employment of men and women?

2. In what ways does technology affect the growth of employment in these two sectors?

3. How might differences in productivity growth in the goods and services sectors affect employment?

The Rising Skill Set

Employment by Selected Occupations

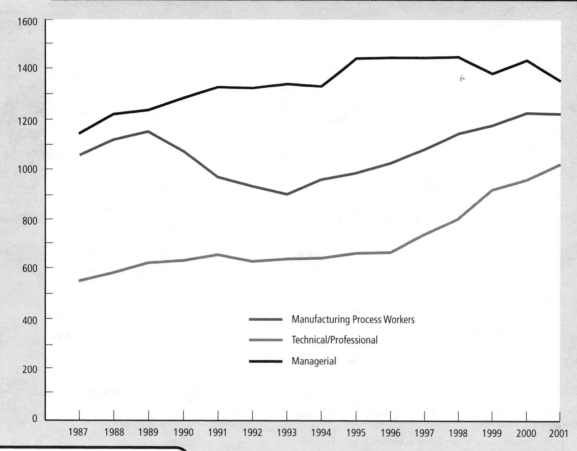

Employment
(thousands)

Legend:
— Manufacturing Process Workers
····· Technical/Professional
— Managerial

Source: Adapted from Statistics Canada/CANSIM (D989543, D989536, D989534).

The common perception that the economy is largely producing low-skilled jobs is incorrect. Primarily, the growth in employment has been in professional occupations, only several of which are illustrated. Professional workers outnumber manufacturing process workers (factory workers), a trend that is likely to continue. This advance in skill requirements is a result of **rising competition** that demands higher standards of performance and the increasing level of technical complexity in today's jobs. The number of managers is also a response to the competitive conditions.

1. Why did the number of manufacturing workers fall and then start to rise? Is this increase going to continue?

2. Why have the technical professional occupations risen so quickly?

3. What factors have caused managerial occupations to fall since 1999?

Figure 72 How Smart Are We?

Employment by Educational Attainment

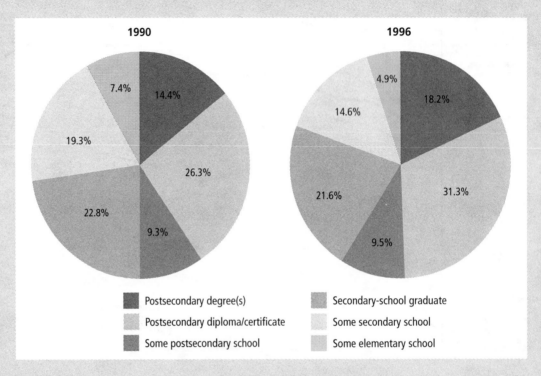

1990

14.4%
7.4%
19.3%
26.3%
22.8%
9.3%

1996

4.9%
18.2%
14.6%
31.3%
21.6%
9.5%

Postsecondary degree(s)

Postsecondary diploma/certificate

Some postsecondary school

Secondary-school graduate

Some secondary school

Some elementary school

Source: Adapted from Statistics Canada, *Labour Force Annual Averages*, 1990, 1996, 71-220-XPB.

As **competition** increases and **technology** becomes more complex, the marketplace demands a higher standard of job performance. Education, together with **experience**, becomes essential for a worker to be able to deliver the increased **productivity** that ensures a high demand for the worker's labour. Contrary to popular belief, the economy is not producing a preponderance of low-skilled jobs. The increasing demand for education challenges the public sector to allocate enough resources to an activity whose payoff to the labour market occurs in the future. Demands on the private resources of students and their families also continue to mount.

1. What are the job prospects for those who cannot or will not pursue more education? Poor jobs or no jobs?

2. What is the re-employment value of secondary-school (high-school) graduation?

3. In what sense does increasing educational attainment reflect the adaptability of society?

4. Is the challenge just a matter of more education, or does it also mean different education than in the past?

Figure 73 Men and Women

Employment by Gender

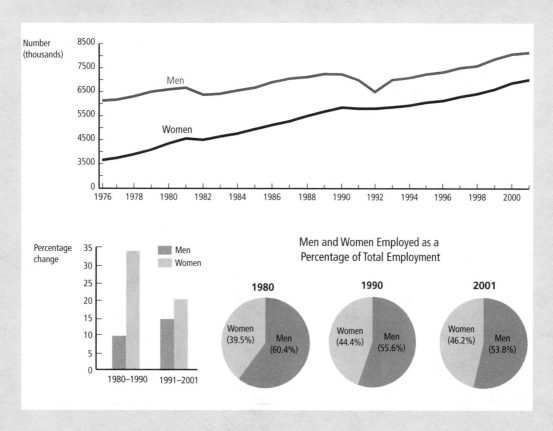

Source: Adapted from Statistics Canada/CANSIM (D980595, D980602, D980609).

In the past women faced unfair **discrimination** in the workplace, and although the situation is improving, it is not yet fully resolved. However, it is clear that the number of women working in the **paid labour force** has risen at a faster rate than has male employment. This has increased the proportion of women as a percentage of those employed. Women are now nearly **equal partners** with men in generating Canada's output. As the relative number of women working rises and as they move into positions of responsibility, discriminatory practices should continue to abate.

1. What has caused so many women to join the paid labour force?

2. Are women working disproportionately in certain industries or occupations?

3. What discriminatory barriers remain?

Figure 74 Young and Old

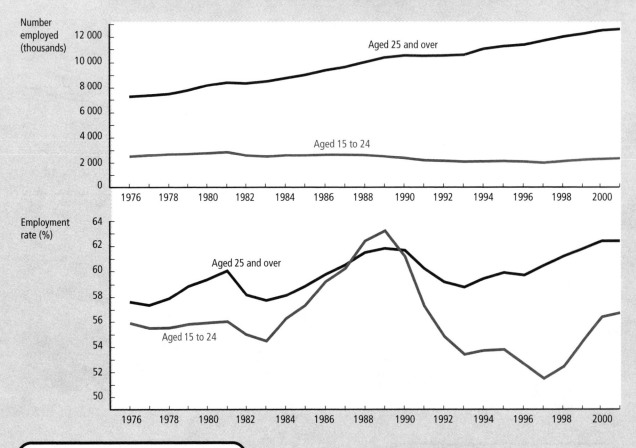

Employment by Age

Source: Statistics Canada/CANSIM (D980800, D980803, D980596, D980599).

A long-term marked difference exists between the growth in employment of those aged 25 and over, and those 15 to 24 years old. "Youth" employment has lagged the employment of the older group by a considerable degree, and it is seen as a pressing **social and economic** problem. However, in a modern, **technologically complex** economy, progressively fewer jobs are available for the uneducated; few jobs are available for teenagers, regardless of how steadily the economy grows. The limited prospects for youth employment are the marketplace's way of telling young persons to pursue their **education**. As the employment rate makes clear, a slightly higher proportion of youth are employed in 2001 than were in 1976, even though the number employed has fallen.

1. How well is the growing demand for highly skilled workers understood? And the falling demand for unskilled workers?

2. How many young people pursue postsecondary education?

3. Why does Statistics Canada start to measure "youth" employment at 15 years?

4. How can the number of youth working fall even though the employment rate rises?

Figure **75**

Too Many Public Servants? Or Too Few?

Public and Private Employment as a Percentage of Total Employment

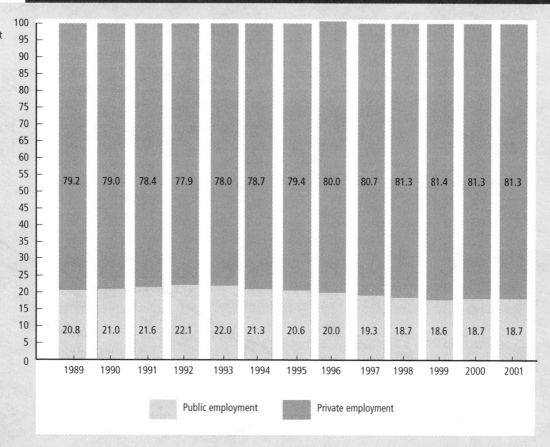

Percentage of total employment

Year	Private employment	Public employment
1989	79.2	20.8
1990	79.0	21.0
1991	78.4	21.6
1992	77.9	22.1
1993	78.0	22.0
1994	78.7	21.3
1995	79.4	20.6
1996	80.0	20.0
1997	80.7	19.3
1998	81.3	18.7
1999	81.4	18.6
2000	81.3	18.7
2001	81.3	18.7

Public employment   Private employment

Source: Adapted from Statistics Canada/CANSIM (D980653, D980595).

Note: Private employment includes business proprietors.

Debate continues about how many public servants Canada needs. This discussion is also related to the appropriate levels of **taxation** and **public spending**, and to the overall role of the public sector. Some argue that several public functions do not deliver **social value** and that others functions can be delivered more **efficiently** by the private marketplace. However, many people see **health care, education,** and **environmental protection**, for example, as high social priorities requiring extensive public involvement.

1. Why did the proportion of public servants fall during the later 1990s?

2. What are "public goods"? Why is the provision of public goods consistent with the theory of the private marketplace?

3. How should the appropriate number of public servants be determined?

Figure 76 Who Creates Jobs Faster?

Rate of Employment Change in Canada and the United States, 1976–2000

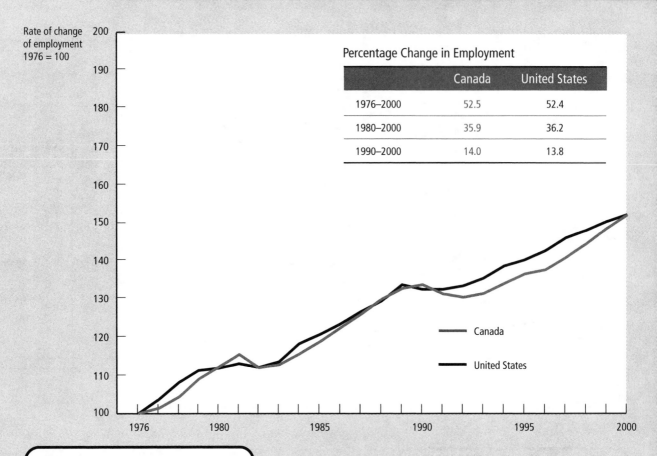

Rate of change of employment 1976 = 100

Percentage Change in Employment

	Canada	United States
1976–2000	52.5	52.4
1980–2000	35.9	36.2
1990–2000	14.0	13.8

Source: Adapted from Statistics Canada/CANSIM (B53104, D980595).

Note: Number employed in 1976 set at 100.

The rate at which an economy can offer employment to its residents is a partial reflection of its success. It is natural to compare Canada's **rate of job creation** with that of its principal **trading partner**. The two economies have similarities and differences with respect to their size, **public policies, rates of GDP growth, rates of population growth,** and **participation rates**, among other factors. The *net* effect of these factors is instructive.

1. Why does the rate of growth in employment in Canada and the United States rise at such a similar rate over such long periods?

2. Why are many Canadians unaware of this fact?

3. Why does employment fall in 1982 and 1991 in both countries? And in 1992 in Canada?

4. How closely linked are the two economies? Does this link predate the Canada–U.S. Free Trade Agreement?

Figure 77 Labour Market Benchmarks

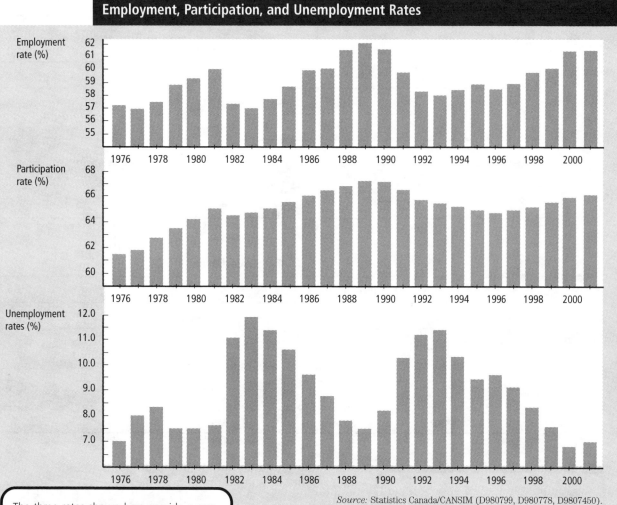

Employment, Participation, and Unemployment Rates

Source: Statistics Canada/CANSIM (D980799, D980778, D9807450).

The three rates shown here provide a comprehensive view of the conditions in **Canada's labour market**. All three are necessary to understand both the strength of individual job opportunities and the overall state of the economy. The employment rate shows the number of people working in the paid labour force as a percentage of those of "working" age (over 15 years). The participation rate measures the number of people in the labour force (including both employed and unemployed) as a proportion of the working-age population. The unemployment rate is the percentage of the labour force that is looking for work. The employment rate is the most affected by economic conditions. The other two rates are driven by economic, social, and demographic factors, for example, the desire to go to school rather than to work in paid employment.

1. What social factors affect the above rates?
2. Why did the unemployment rate increase sharply in the early 1980s and the early 1990s? Why did it fall subsequently?
3. Why did the participation and employment rates fall, only to begin to rise again?

Figure 78 Why Should You Like Your Work?

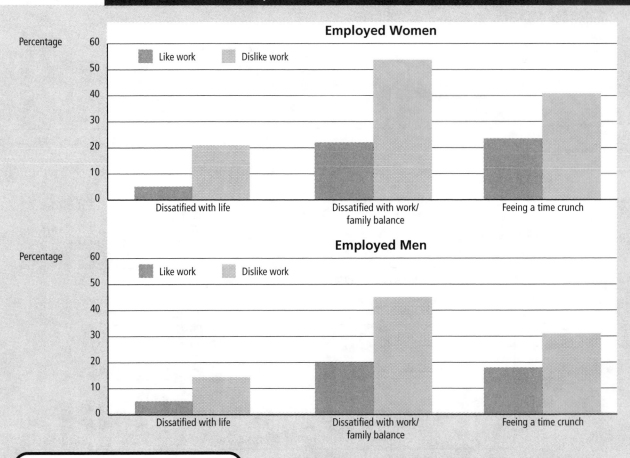

The Relationship between Attitude to Work and Attitude to Life

Employed Women

Percentage

Like work   Dislike work

Dissatified with life   Dissatified with work/ family balance   Feeing a time crunch

Employed Men

Percentage

Like work   Dislike work

Dissatified with life   Dissatified with work/ family balance   Feeing a time crunch

Source: Statistics Canada, *Enjoying Work: An Effective Strategy in the Struggle to Juggle*, Canadian Social Trends, Summer 2001 (11-008).

Some people do not believe it is necessary to like their work, that the income from employment is satisfaction enough. Research, however, shows that the enjoyment of work plays an important part in a person's overall sense of satisfaction or **welfare**. For women, a very strong relationship exists between dissatisfaction with work and dissatisfaction with life, and between the balance between work and family and an increased sense of a time crunch. A similar effect exists for men, although to a lesser degree.

1. What causes dissatisfaction with work to affect such quality of life issues as satisfaction with life, work–family balance, and a sense of a time crunch?

2. Why would the relationship among these issues be of a lesser consequence for men?

3. What effect does enjoying work have on productivity?

Figure **79** How Good Is the Worker?

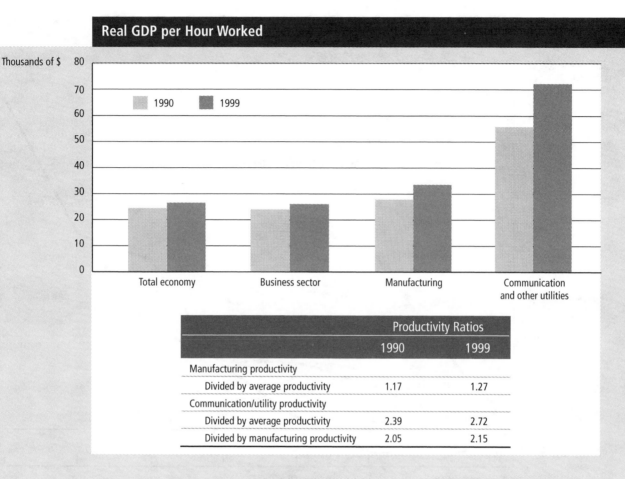

Real GDP per Hour Worked

	Productivity Ratios	
	1990	1999
Manufacturing productivity		
Divided by average productivity	1.17	1.27
Communication/utility productivity		
Divided by average productivity	2.39	2.72
Divided by manufacturing productivity	2.05	2.15

Source: Adapted from Statistics Canada/CANSIM (I602501, I602605, I602608, I602502, I602510).

Note: Productivity is measured as output per hour worked.

Real GDP per hour worked is a measure of **productivity** and varies substantially among the various sectors and subsectors of the economy. In 1990 **communications and utility** workers contributed more than twice as much output as did the average worker in the overall economy. **Manufacturing workers** add more output than does the average worker and the average worker in the business sector. These differences *strengthened* through to 1999. Both manufacturing and communications/utilities increased their lead over the total economy, and communications/utilities increased its lead over manufacturing.

1. What factors produce such dramatic differences in productivity between both manufacturing and communications/utilities and the total economy, and between manufacturing and communications/utilities?

2. Why might these differences continue into the future? Why might they stop?

3. Why do these productivity measurements present only a very limited view of the economy?

Figure How Fast Are Workers Getting Better?

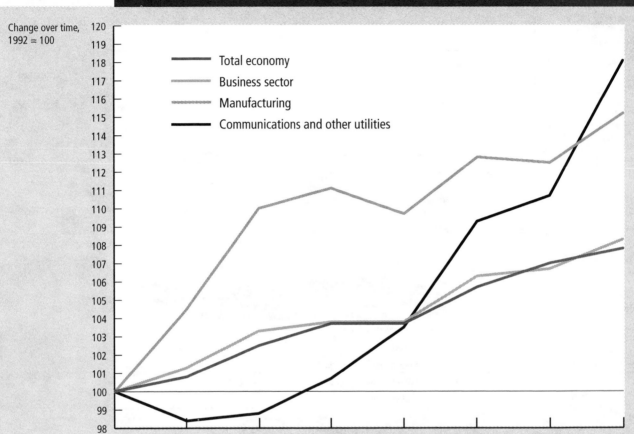

GDP per Hour Worked

Change over time, 1992 = 100

Legend:
- Total economy
- Business sector
- Manufacturing
- Communications and other utilities

Source: Adapted from Statistics Canada/CANSIM (I602501, I602605, I602608, I602502, I602510).

From 1992 to 1999, **productivity** in manufacturing and communications both grew faster than did that for the overall economy and for the **business sector**. Although productivity for the overall economy did rise over the period, the growth stopped in 1996 and then resumed. Note that this graph shows the rate of change for output per hour, while Figure 79 showed the magnitudes.

1. Why did the productivity in manufacturing and communications/utilities rise faster than that of the business sector and the overall economy? Why did communications/utilities outgrow manufacturing? Is the answer to the question necessarily the same as the one for question 1 for Figure 79?

2. Why might these different growth rates continue? How can technological innovation be predicted?

3. What part do demand conditions play in these observations about productivity?

4. How might these productivity numbers have affected the stock market, especially the NASDAQ? (See Figure 40.)

5. Why are the productivity growth figures for the total economy and the business sector so similar? Why did they both pause in 1996?

Figure

Who Gets the Raises?

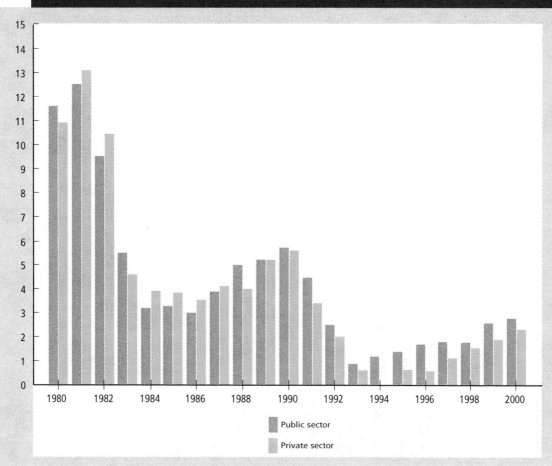

Wage Settlements

Rate of wage settlement

Public sector

Private sector

Source: Adapted from Statistics Canada, *Perspectives on Labour and Income*, Autumn 2000, Vol. 12, no. 3, "Unionization—An Update." Available at <http://www.statcan.ca>.

All employees are naturally concerned with wage increases. Since wages in general reflect the **productivity** of the worker, wage increases should be related to productivity increases. However, in many situations, neither the worker nor the employer knows what has actually happened to productivity levels. Considerable controversy exists concerning whether public sector wage settlements are appropriate and the degree to which they affect private sector wage claims.

1. What has caused wage *increases* to both slow and accelerate over this period?

2. Why did wages fall so sharply in 1983 and never match the previous increases?

3. Why are the increases since 1992 low compared to the previous period?

4. Does it appear that public sector wages increases are disproportionate to those of the private sector?

Figure 82 Working or Not?

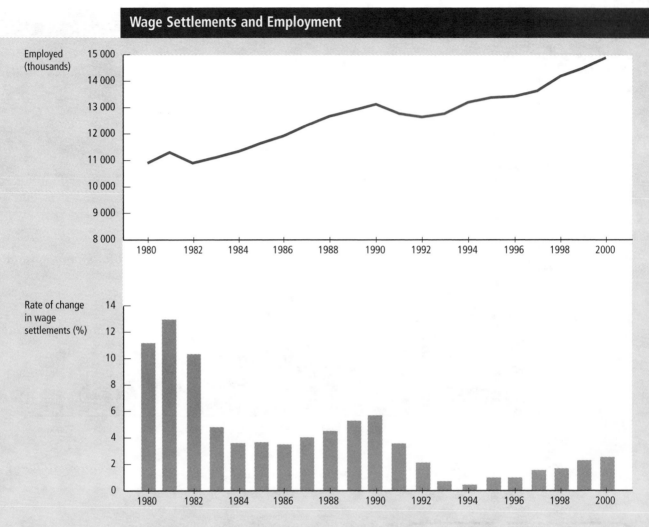

Wage Settlements and Employment

Source: Adapted from Statistics Canada/CANSIM (D980595) and *Perspectives on Labour and Income*, Autumn 2000, Vol. 12, no. 3, "Unionization—An Update." Available at <http://www.statcan.ca>.

The willingness of workers to press for high wage settlements is affected by their sense of how easy it is to find a job and how many people are unemployed. If it is easy for a worker to find a job, it is therefore *harder* for an employer to hire. **Negotiating power** should be higher for workers when the **unemployment rate** is low and **employment** is rising, and higher for the employers when the reverse is true. But this balance of power is only part of the answer, since historical benchmarks, productivity, and other issues may also affect large settlements. Many workers do not negotiate their wages in a collective bargaining (union) context.

1. Why were labour market conditions weak in the early 1980s and early 1990s?

2. Is the connection between wage settlements and overall employment becoming closer or not?

3. What proportion of workers negotiates their wages in collective (union) agreements?

Figure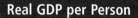

Canada's Standard of Living

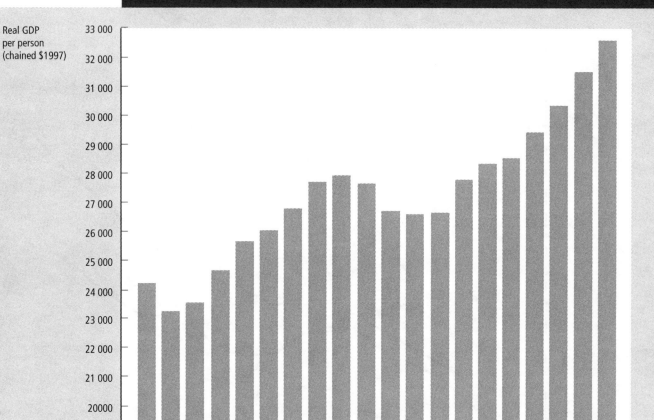

Real GDP per Person

Real GDP per person (chained $1997)

Source: Statistics Canada/CANSIM (D100126, D1).

Canada's **standard of living** can be captured by a variety of indicators. Real GDP per person is one of the broadest measures, even though it excludes a number of elements, among them the **distribution of income** and various intangible considerations. By using GDP per person, the contribution to **welfare** by both the private and the public sectors is included. GDP per person, of course, does not rise every year and is a function of both **economic performance** and population trends. For this measure of standard of living to rise, the economy must advance faster than the **rate of growth of the population**. Performance is determined by **macroeconomic policy**, **external economic conditions**, and the **rate of growth of productivity**.

1. Why did the standard of living fall in 1982 and from 1990 to 1992?

2. Why does the standard of living rise *most* years?

3. Why do many Canadians seem to think that the standard of living has not risen to a record high?

Figure Whose Standard of Living Rises Faster?

Rate of GDP Growth per Person: Canada and the United States

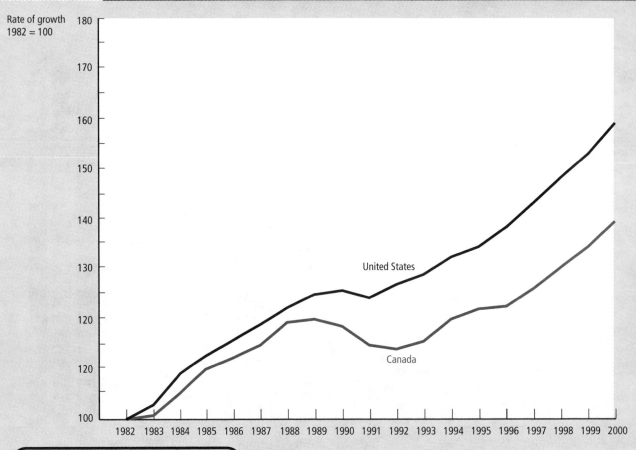

Rate of growth
1982 = 100

Source: Adapted from Statistics Canada/CANSIM (D100126, D1, D369455), and The Federal Bank of St. Louis, *Monthly Employment and Population Data*, Available at <www.stls.frb.org/fred/data/employ.html>.

The standards of living in Canada and the United States, as measured by GDP per person, have risen significantly over this period. The Canadian standard is up more than 40 percent and that of the United States up almost 60 percent. The difference in these two rates is significant. Part of this difference results from the fact that Canada's **population** grew faster than that of the United States, 22.5 percent compared to the U.S. population increase of 18.5 percent. (These figures do not consider illegal immigration.) Part of the difference results from the fact that the U.S. economy grew more quickly than Canada's during this period. Of course, these measures do not account for differences in the **distribution of income** and other **intangible considerations**.

1. What are the factors that cause this difference in growth in the standard of living? Is it a function of technology or resources or public policy?

2. How might those factors be changed to speed the increase in Canada's standard of living?

3. To what extent would differences in the distribution of income between Canadian and the United States affect GDP per person as a measurement of *average* welfare?

4. What other intangible considerations might modify these observations?

Figure 85 Another Way to Measure the Standard of Living

Real per Person Disposable Income

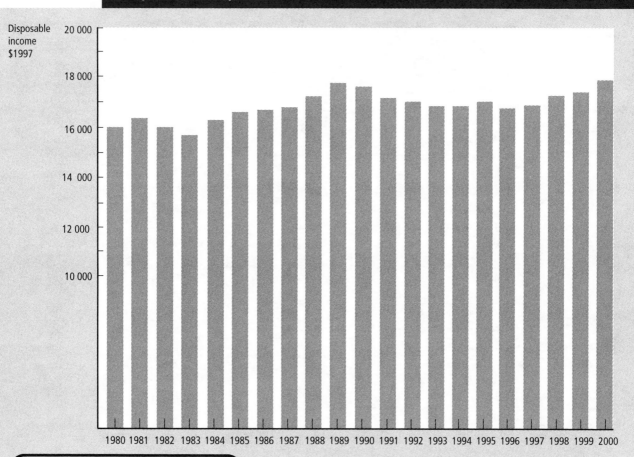

Disposable income $1997

Source: Adapted from Statistics Canada/CANSIM (D22512, D1, P100000).

Real disposable income per person measures the **purchasing power** of income after the effects of **inflation** and **direct taxation** are removed. This statistic must be used very carefully because it excludes the value of all **public goods and services**, both tangible and intangible. In this sense, it is not a complete description of the **standard of living**; however, it is still a useful indicator, especially of consumer spending that is closely related to disposable income. Real disposable income is also a factor that affects **consumer confidence**. Note that the record high of disposable income per person achieved in the late 1980s was not reached again until the start of the 2000s. The erosion during the 1990s was the result of the **recession** of 1990–91, the slow growth that followed in the early 1990s, and population growth.

1. Why did real disposable income recover faster after the recession of 1981–82 than after 1990–91?

2. What role did reduced public spending play in slowing the recovery of disposable income in the 1990s?

3. What was the effect of monetary policy on disposable income during the 1990s?

86 How Much Stuff Do We Own?

Household Ownership by Categories of Possessions (by Percentage of Households)

Type of Possession	Ownership by Percentage of Household		
	1997	1990	1980
TOTAL HOUSEHOLDS	100	100	100
RESIDENCE			
Owned	64.3	63.7	64.3
With mortgage	33.6	31.2	36.1
Without mortgage	30.7	32.5	28.2
Rented	35.7	36.3	35.7
TYPE OF DWELLING			
Single detached	56.7	57.3	57.8
Single attached	10.2	8.2	8.1
Other	33.0	34.5	33.5
HOUSEHOLDS WITH			
Bath facilities	99.8	99.4	98.3
One bath and shower	67.3	NA	NA
Two or more	32.5	NA	NA
Flush toilets	99.8	99.5	98.8
One flush toilet	54.1	59.7	69.8
Two or more	45.7	39.8	29.0
HEATING AND EQUIPMENT			
Furnace	66.7	67.5	75.5
Other	33.3	32.5	24.5
HEATING FUEL			
Oil	13.1	17.6	37.6
Gas	48.7	44.6	39.7
Electricity	34.4	33.1	19.5
Other	3.7	4.7	3.1
FUEL FOR COOKING			
Electricity	93.5	93.8	99.1
Gas	6.2	5.4	8.7
Other	0.3	0.7	2.2
ELECTRIC WASHING MACHINE			
Automatic	78.3	75.1	64.8
Other	1.4	3.5	12.9
HOUSEHOLDS WITH			
Clothes dryers	76.7	73.4	63.6
Dishwashers	48.5	42.0	28.5
Refrigerators	99.8	99.5	NA
Freezers	55.9	57.6	51.0
Microwave ovens	86.3	68.2	NA
Gas barbecues	53.9	44.6	NA

(cont.)

Type of Possession	Ownership by Percentage of Household		
	1997	1990	1980
TOTAL HOUSEHOLDS	100	100	100
Air conditioners	29.1	24.4	16.6
Smoke detectors	96.1	86.3	NA
Portable fire extinguishers	53.1	45.1	NA
Telephones	98.6	98.5	NA
Radios			
One	17.6	18.7	NA
Two or more	81.1	80.3	NA
Cassette or tap recoders	82.0	67.4	48.4
Compact disc player	58.1	15.4	NA
Cable TV	73.7	71.3	54.4
Video recorders	84.7	66.3	NA
Camcorders	17.7	5.6	NA
Home computers	36.0	16.3	NA
Television sets			
One	46.8	57.5	NA
Two or more	51.9	39.4	NA
Black and white only	0.4	2.1	16.6
OWNED VEHICLES			
One	43.4	44.1	NA
Two or more	39.8	39.1	NA
OWNED AUTOMOBILES			
One	52.3	53.1	53.8
Two or more	20.1	24.7	26.1
OWNED VANS AND TRUCKS	32.8	23.4	NA

Source: Statistics Canada (13-218-XBP): Household Facilities by Income and Other Characteristics (1997).

Note: NA = not available—not measured by Statistics Canada.

The ownership of homes and **consumer durables** can be used as an indicator of the **standard of living**, if interpreted carefully and in context. These observations are the reflection of **consumer expenditures** and those for **residential construction**. They also can be used to evaluate whether the **retail market** for a particular durable will enjoy strong or weak **demand**. Both **macroeconomic** and **microeconomic issues** are involved.

1. Why is it important to look at the proportion of households who own certain things, rather than just the *number* of households who have them?

2. Why did the proportion of households owning a colour television fall?

3. Do these figures reflect any sign of widespread economic distress? How complete a picture of household affluence do these figures represent?

4. Why is the strongest demand for microwave ovens likely over?

Figure

How Equal Is the Distribution of Income?

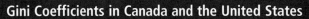

Gini Coefficients in Canada and the United States

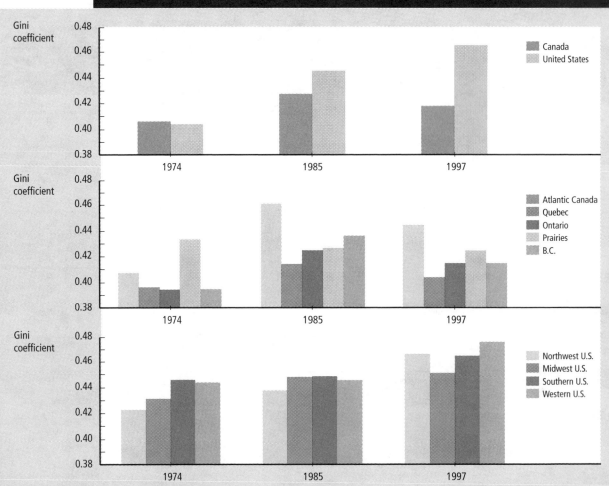

Source: Adapted from Statistics Canada, *Canadian Economic Observer*, "Income Inequity in North America," August 2000.

Average or mean income can be misleading since it does not take into account the distribution of income across the range of income. In this regard, Canada and the United States exhibit sharply different conditions. A common way to measure inequality in the **distribution of income** is the **Gini coefficient**. This value ranges from 0 (perfect equality: everyone has same share) to 1 (perfect inequality: one person has it all). In other words, the higher the value, the greater the inequality. Using the Gini coefficient, it is clear that the distribution of income is more unequally divided in the United States compared to Canada. Moreover, income inequality in the United States has increased throughout the period noted. Although inequality did increase in Canada from 1974 to 1985, since 1985 it has been improving (the Gini coefficient is falling.) As a result, correcting for differences in **purchasing power** between Canada and the United States, Canadians in the bottom third of the income ranking have purchasing power higher than or equal to their U.S. counterparts. It also means that those in the top ranking in the United States had a significantly higher income than their counterparts in Canada. Regionally, all regions in the United States showed an increase in inequality from 1974 to 1997. In Canada, all the regions showed improvement from 1985 forward.

1. Why are there persistent and significant differences in the distribution of income between Canada and the United States?

2. Why did the degree of inequality in Canada fall from 1985 to 1997?

3. What role has Canada's trading relationship with the United States played in regard to the distribution of income?

4. What effects could result if the inequality in distribution of income in the United States continues to increase?

Figure

88 Where Is It Cheapest to Live?

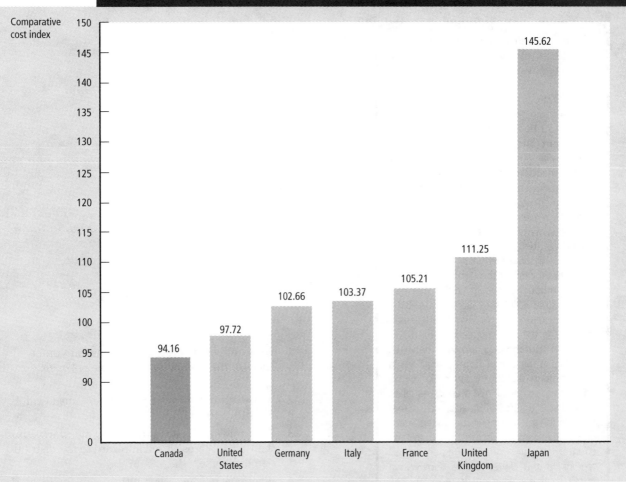

Cost of Living Comparisons

Comparative cost index

Countries (left to right): Canada 94.16, United States 97.72, Germany 102.66, Italy 103.37, France 105.21, United Kingdom 111.25, Japan 145.62

Source: World Competitiveness Yearbook, June 2000, p. 369. Prepared by the International Institute for Management Development, Lausanne, Switzerland.

Since it is difficult to measure differences in the **standard of living** among countries, it is helpful to look at the situation from different perspectives. Instead of just looking at what **income** someone receives, it is useful to note that the **cost of living** varies among countries. This variation is influenced by the **microeconomic conditions** in each country. Their cost of living can affect both **individual welfare** and **international economic competitiveness**.

1. Why does the cost of living vary so much among these countries?

2. Is there a relationship between cost of living and the pace of economic activity?

Conclusion: Making Economic Connections

The selections of statistical evidence in this textbook are intended to address one overriding theme: they present historical evidence solely to help you look forward. We must ask whether the economy will adapt to future demands. That it has adapted successfully in response to serious difficulties in the past is clear: both destabilizing inflation and unsustainable deficits were eliminated, and the degree of the success was credible both from the perspective of past accomplishments and the standards of other countries. Yet no one would deny that the responses could have been improved in speed, effectiveness, and efficiency. By carefully understanding how Canadian society has adapted to yesterday's challenges, we can have confidence in the future *and* insight into how to adapt even more successfully. Competition is driving the standard of performance ever higher.

Statistical Sources—Suggested Sites for Economic Data

- Bank of Canada: www.bankofcanada.ca/en/
  The best source for Canadian financial data. Click on *Weekly Financial Statistics* for up-to-date statistics. *About the Bank* gives an overview of the Bank's history and operations, and *Publications and Research* contains economic reports.

- Statistics Canada: www.statcan.ca/start.html
  The best source for Canadian economic data. Click on *Daily News* for updated information and newly released studies. Click on *Canadian Statistics* for demographic and economic data.

- Organisation for Economic Co-operation and Development: www.oecd.org
  The best source for international statistics. Click on *Statistics* and *Economic statistics*.

- Department of Finance: www.fin.gc.ca/fin-eng.html
  Good background information on the Canadian budget and public debt. This site contains lots of information but has some key material under *Budget Info* and *Publications*.

- Canoe (Canadian Online Explorer): www.canoe.ca
  A large Canadian News site. It contains links to major newspapers and magazines, and also carries the daily headlines. Very easy to navigate.

- Via University Libraries

    Statistics Canada's CANSIM database

    Lexis Nexis, if available

A Guide to Using this Book with Pearson Introductory Economics Texts

Readers are encouraged to search out the information and analysis they need to answer the questions attached to each unit. These are real-world questions and you should not look for simple, self-contained answers. The textbooks that are listed below can provide general guidance on all the answers, but they will only help you to find the answer; they do not necessarily provide the full answer. Besides using the textbooks' indexes, you will find the topics addressed specifically in the chapters indicated in the table on page 98.

- *Canadian Microeconomics: Problems and Policies*
  Brian Lyons
- *Economics Today: The Micro View*
  Roger LeRoy Miller, Brenda Abbott, Sam Fefferman, Ronald K. Kessler, and Terrence Sulyma
- *Principles of Microeconomics*
  Karl E. Case, Ray C. Fair, J. Frank Strain, and Michael R. Veall
- *Working with Economics: A Canadian Framework*
  H. Richard Hird
- *Principles of Macroeconomics*
  Karl E. Case, Ray C. Fair, J. Frank Strain, and Michael R. Veall
- *Canadian Macroeconomics: Problems and Policies*
  Brian Lyons
- *Macroeconomics: Principles and Tools*
  Arthur O'Sullivan, Steven M. Sheffrin, and Rob Moir
- *Economics*
  Richard Lipsey and Christopher T.S. Ragan

	Micro Lyons	Micro Miller	Micro Case	Working Hird	Macro Case	Macro Lyons	Macro O'Sullivan	Economics Lipsey
PART I								
GDP	1	1, 2	1, 2, 22	1, 5, 6	1, 2, 6, 7	1, 2, 6	1, 2, 5, 6, 8	1, 20, 32
Industrial Sectors	3	20	3	10	3	4	9	
Foreign Trade	4		4	9	20, 21	9, 10, 11	4, 16	34, 35, 36
PART II								
Profit and Investments	2, 3, 8	7, 14	7	2				7, 8
Prices	4, 5, 6, 7	4, 5, 8, 20	4, 7	2	4		9	3, 4
Cost of Business	8	10	8, 9	11	5			7, 8
Entrepreneurship	3	2	4					
Technology	5, 7	20	7	13				8
PART III								
Stock Markets	6	9, 11	4, 5, 7, 11	7, 12	11, 12	5	11	9, 16
Interest Rates				7	11, 12	6, 7	12, 13	26, 27, 28
Average Prices				6, 7	8, 14	6, 7, 8, 13	12, 13, 14, 15	26, 27, 28, 29
Balance Sheet		9			16	5	12	27
Public Finances	12	6	3, 16, 18	3, 4	10		18	12, 18, 31
PART IV								
Employment	10, 11	15, 16	14	14	8, 15		7, 15	14, 30
Productivity and Wages	10	15	5	5	19	3, 8		14
Standard of Living	14	18, 19	5	5	7		5	17, 2